THE LEADER'S CHARACTER

2nd Edition

DR. GREGORY L. CRUELL

WESTBOW
PRESS®
A DIVISION OF THOMAS NELSON
& ZONDERVAN

WestBow Press books may be ordered through booksellers or by contacting:

WestBow Press
A Division of Thomas Nelson & Zondervan
1663 Liberty Drive
Bloomington, IN 47403
www.westbowpress.com
844-714-3454

Scripture taken from the King James Version of the Bible

ISBN: 978-1-6642-8870-6 (sc)
ISBN: 978-1-6642-8868-3 (hc)
ISBN: 978-1-6642-8869-0 (e)

Library of Congress Control Number: 2023900319

Print information available on the last page.

WestBow Press rev. date: 02/24/2023

CONTENTS

Session III: Proven Principles of Character Development

Session IV: The Other Side of Failure

ACKNOWLEDGMENTS

I would like to thank all of the leaders and laborers, both past and present, with whom I have served and who have lived the principles of this book in conduct and deed. Your influence has made a difference in my life and in the development of the Ethnos Leadership Process. I am grateful for the relationships that we share, because "without a relationship, there is no leadership."

To my precious wife for life and best friend, Deirdre, who has been as Barnabas was to Paul, my God-sent encourager: your love and support have made me a better leader. Thank you.

To my children, Nicole, Stephanie, and Genese, you have been created to make a difference in the world. Always remember that you are Ethnos (people-centered) leaders.

To the reader, it is our sincere desire that as you read *The Leader's Character*, which is the first of three books that help to facilitate the Ethnos Leadership Process, you will discover in these pages additional tools and truth that will assist you in your lifetime leadership journey, which will make a difference in the world.

> Almost every successful person begins with two beliefs: the future can be better than the present, and I have the power to make it so.
> —David Brooks

THE WHAT AND WHY OF ETHNOS LEADERSHIP

Leadership and mentorship are opposite sides of the same coin. For leadership to be authentic, there must be mentorship; you cannot have one without the other. Our philosophy concerning this concept is seen in what we call the Ethnos Equation:

Mentorship: Purposeful Relationships +Authentic Accountability = Professional Responsibility

Merriam-Webster's Dictionary defines a profession or professionalism as "the conduct, aims, or qualities that characterize or mark a particular profession." This definition implies that professionalism encompasses a number of different attributes and that together, these attributes identify and define a professional.

Mentorship is the non-negotiable epicenter of Ethnos Leadership. Mentorship in Ethnos Leadership is the *professional responsibility* that is acquired and required for organizational health and well-being. At every level in an organization, the leader and the led need a mentor for *accountability*.

Purposeful relationships are valued, trusted, and respected. Bonds or alliances of this manner open the door to forthright accountability. Being accountable or answerable to a trusted friend, adviser, or mentor provides both protection and correction through life and leadership in an environment that is safe because it is trusted and valued.

Responsibility simply means cultivating one's ability to respond to the distinct circumstances and situations of one's personal and organizational leadership influence via the Ethnos Leadership Process (discover, develop, disciple, make a difference).

The leader's professional responsibility is learned and acquired through the evolution of intentional mentorship by virtue of purposeful relationships. Purposeful relationships are rooted in the principle attributed to Saint Francis of Assisi: "Seek first to understand rather than to be understood." Understanding the organization's goals and the people or team that make the organization function and grow are informed by this basic universal principle.

The word *nations* in the original Greek is *ethnos*. Ethnos may be defined as "a group of people bound together by the same customs, conduct, language, behaviors, or other distinguishing features."

Ethnos Leadership is a principle-centered, self-evaluating, self-reflective leadership development process synergized by a commitment to being and becoming a lifelong learner and leader who is determined to make a difference. Our definition of a principle at Ethnos Leadership is "a universal law that is true in any context, situation, or environment." Ethnos Leadership is a blueprint to reinforce, strengthen, and sharpen existing leadership skills by expanding one's perspective of leadership.

This concept is applicable to a person who has been leading for many years or to one who is just beginning the leadership journey. Ethnos Leadership is comprised of three modules—character, capabilities, and competencies—and each module has four sessions.

At the conclusion of each individual session, participants will create a summary that outlines the principles discovered and a plan for developing these principles. This aspect of the Ethnos Leadership Process is the Personal Leadership Perspective (PLP).

During the forty-hour process, participants will combine their twelve Personal Leadership Perspective summaries to create a cumulative plan or writing of the Personal Leadership Character Story (PLCS), which initiates the final phase of the process, titled "Commitment to Investing in Personal and Organizational Transformation."

The platform is grounded emphatically in self-evaluation and self-reflection. The conclusion of the process is the commitment to a lifetime of discovering, developing, and "disciple-ing" those we lead who are bound together by the Ethnos Leadership Process, thus making a difference across nations and ethnicities.

This book contains the four sessions of the character module, which encourage the leader to continue discovering the limitless dimensions of expanding one's character by looking in the mirror, or self-reflection. *Character* refers to a person's ethical and moral traits. These traits can be used to assist the leader in developing his or her individuality. The behavior of a leader is directed by the character traits of the leader. The character of a person is evident, no matter what the situation. Behavior can change, but the nature of character does not.

The final forming of a person's character lies in their own hands.

—Anne Frank

For more information about Ethnos Leadership and the Ethnos Leadership Process, contact us via email at info@gregorycruell.com or by phone at (619) 765-4868.

SESSION I

CHARACTER AND VIRTUE: THE FOUNDATIONS OF AUTHENTIC LEADERSHIP

Foundation

The purpose of this session is to discuss character and virtue, the foundations of authentic leadership. Character and virtue are components of an authentic leader's quest for a lifetime commitment to leadership development that makes a difference, both personally and organizationally. A Google search of *leadership development* produces 91,300,000 results. A plethora of information concerning leadership development is available to us today. However, if you take one thousand people, place them in a room, and ask them for one word that could define, describe, or possibly be agreed upon concerning leadership, that one word would be *influence*.

The National Leadership Index, compiled by the Center for Public Leadership at Harvard University's John F. Kennedy School of Government, demonstrates that America's confidence in her leaders has been significantly below average for the third year in a row.[1] The report on the index findings, *A National Study of Confidence*

---

[1] S. A. Rosenthal, *National Leadership Index 2012: A National Study of Confidence in Leadership*, Center for Public Leadership, Harvard Kennedy School, Harvard University, Cambridge, Massachusetts.

in Leadership, found that over the six-year history of the survey, the dominant trend has been the majority view that America has a leadership crisis and a concomitant declining confidence in leadership. The study looks beyond political leadership to encompass twelve major sectors of leadership in America.

- Military
- Medical
- Nonprofit and charity
- Supreme Court
- Local government
- Religious
- Education
- Executive branch
- State government
- News media
- Congress
- Wall Street

In 2012, the study indicated that the United States military has the highest confidence level of leadership among American citizens. Nonetheless, according to the 2012 study, 69 percent of Americans still believe there is a leadership crisis.[2]

Les Csorba, in his book *Trust: the One Thing That Makes or Breaks a Leader,* says "leadership is character in motion."[3] Csorba goes on to say in his introduction that trust has been shattered in many of our political, ecclesiastical, corporate, financial, familial, and media institutions.[4] We are reminded frequently on the internet and in local newscasts of our current leadership crisis. This is a reminder to the world in which we live that *character matters.*

The suggestion in this session is that the answer to this leadership

---

[2] Ibid.
[3] Les T. Csorba, *Trust: The One Thing That Makes or Breaks a Leader* (Nashville, TN: Thomas Nelson Publishers, 2004), xxiii.
[4] Ibid.

crisis is consistent and persistent development of character and virtue, the foundations of authentic leadership. Not everyone will become the CEO of a Fortune 500 company, nor will everyone be recognized on national television as a war hero or the leader of an organization that discovers the next world-changing technological breakthrough of the century. Yet there are quiet leaders all around us. We know them as our wives and husbands, sons and daughters, coworkers and neighbors, police officers and firefighters, emergency service personnel, our children's teachers—great men and women who are making a historical difference in our society because of their influence.

I attribute influence to the ethical values of character and virtue that a person possesses individually, which affects each community, collectively. Yourdictionary.com's definition of *influence* states that it is "the capacity of persons or things to become a compelling force that effects the actions, behavior and conduct of others."

Within this definition, the phrase *compelling force* is particularly noteworthy. The word *compelling* means "having a powerful and irresistible effect," while the word *force* suggests the "strength or power exerted upon an object or power and the ability to convince."

The German statesman and poet Johann Wolfgang von Goethe, said, "Behavior is a mirror in which everyone displays his own image."[5] Looking into the mirror of self informs the process of self-discovery that should continue, uninterrupted, daily. Most if not all of us look into a mirror daily. The question that we must ask ourselves continually is, "As a leader, what about me needs to change?"

Change is constant and inevitable—as we age, there is change; as technology grows or improves, there is change; and as we learn more about people, there is change. To resist change is pointless; to understand and embrace change is beneficial.

This session suggests that what produces change in authentic leadership is the development of character and the inculcation of virtues.

---

[5] www.thinkexist.com. Accessed October 12, 2014.

PART I

A PERSPECTIVE ON VIRTUES

The dictionary defines *character* as distinct attributes, qualities, traits, or features that make up and distinguish an individual's behavior and conduct. These qualities usually include moral or emotional traits, such as strength, honesty, and fairness.

In the introduction to his book *Virtuous Leadership: An Agenda for Personal Excellence*, Alexandre Havard stated,

> Character is forged not by codes of ethical conduct, but rather through the cultivation of the virtues of antiquity that have been passed down through the Judeo-Christian tradition. Thus, it shows that leadership and virtue are not only compatible they are actually synonymous. And one's growth as a leader runs parallel to one's growth in virtue.[6]

Havard suggests that it is virtue or, more precisely, the set of classical human virtues (prudence, courage, self-control, and justice) that make up the content of a person's character.[7] Peter Drucker, one of the preeminent management theoreticians of our time said, "It is character through which leadership is exercised." His colleague in the

---

[6] Alexandre Havard, *Virtuous Leadership: An Agenda for Personal Excellence* (New Rochelle, NY: Scepter Publishers, 2007), xiv.
[7] Ibid.

field of management and leadership, Warren Bennis, distinguished professor of business administration and founding chairman of the Leadership Institute at the University of Southern California, stated, "Leadership is a metaphor for centeredness, congruity, and balance in one's life."[8]

Many might argue that character is not something with which we are born; others would agree that character can be shaped, molded, and strengthened. As we do so, we achieve what Bennis declared as centeredness, congruity, and balance in life. Within an organizational structure, to be centered is to know and understand the common goals and values of the organization to which one belongs. Congruity simply means harmony and agreement. Our respective strengths as members of a team provide the quickest and most effective results that ensure success for our company or organization. To speak of balance means to recognize the totality of one's life purpose.

Not only do I have a responsibility to the organization of which I am a part, but if I'm married, I have a responsibility to my wife or husband, and if I have children, I have a responsibility to them. To be balanced means to recognize the value of spiritual well-being: the necessity of eating well, exercising, and getting the proper rest. This all becomes a part of my conduct and behavior that accentuates and solidifies good, sound, moral character, or authentic leadership.

Defining Virtue

Virtue, by definition, is a person's moral excellence. A morally excellent person has a character made up of virtues that are valued as good—for example, virtues such as honesty, respect, courage, forgiveness, and kindness. Because of these virtues or positive character traits, a leader is committed to doing the right thing, no matter the personal cost, and does not bend to impulses, urges, or

---

[8] Ibid, xv.

desires but consistently acts according to the traits and virtuous principles previously mentioned.[9]

The Online Etymology Dictionary states that our English word *virtue* arose in approximately AD 1200 from the Anglo-French and Old French *vertu*,[10] which means force, vigor, moral strength, qualities, and abilities. The tenth-century Old French translation carries the connotation of a moral life and conduct or a particular moral excellence. From the Latin *virtutem* comes the meaning of moral strength, high character, goodness, manliness, valor, bravery, courage (in war), excellence, and worth.[11] Virtues are qualities of the mind, the will, and the heart that instill strength of character and stability of personality.

Plato stated that the four main virtues are *prudence, justice, courage,* and *temperance (self-control).* These are the cardinal virtues of antiquity derived from the Latin word *cardo,* or hinge, and are the virtues upon which all others hinge.[12] Havard suggested that we strengthen our character through the habitual practice of these virtues. In so doing, character leaves an indelible imprint on our temperaments, which then ceases to dominate our personalities.[13] Temperament is regarded as innate or inborn, not learned. It refers to the various aspects of an individual's personality, such as extroversion or introversion. Temperament is also an essential element in a person's emotional activity. Although temperament is said to be a natural instinct, it also can be nurtured as one grows.[14] Personality is defined as a dynamic and organized set of characteristics that a person possesses that has a unique influence on his or her perceptions, motivations, and behaviors in various situations. Thus, personality refers simply to

[9] "What Are Virtues?" Virtues for Life, accessed April 7, 2015, http://www.virtuesforlife.com/what-are-virtues.

[10] "Virtue," Online Etymology Dictionary, accessed October 12, 2014, http://www.etymonline.com.

[11] Ibid.

[12] Havard, *Virtuous Leadership*, xiv.

[13] Ibid.

[14] Difference Between.net, accessed October 12, 2014, http://www.differencebetween.net/language/words-language/difference-between-temperament-and-personality/

individual differences in characteristic patterns of thinking, feeling, and behaving.[15]

From Havard's perspective, it is not one's personality or temperament that should govern character but the habitual practice of the virtues. Havard's position is that such habitual practice of virtues transcends emotions and feelings and therefore develops solid moral character. Havard believes that as each virtue is practiced habitually and progressively, "One's capacity to act or one's conduct or behavior is enhanced for the better."[16]

Prudence

> If we continue to develop our technology without wisdom or prudence, our servant may prove to be our executioner.
>
> —General Omar Bradley

Prudence comes from the Latin *prudentia*, meaning "foresight and sagacity." In Old French, prudence means "wisdom to see what is virtuous, suitable, and profitable."[17] Eric Kessler and James R. Bailey's research states that prudence has at least four important features:

1. Responds to the demands of complex situations
2. Is activated in conflict and contradictory circumstances
3. Includes the whole person (emotions, actions, and personal character)
4. Is learned (or not) over time[18]

---

[15] K. P. L. Hardison, "How Does Personality Differ from Character and Temperament?" Enotes, accessed October 12, 2014, http://www.enotes.com.

[16] Havard, *Virtuous* Leadership, xvi.

[17] "Prudence," Online Etymology Dictionary, accessed April 7, 2015, http://www.etymonline.com.

[18] Eric H. Kessler and James R. Bailey, *Handbook of Organizational and Managerial Wisdom* (Los Angeles, CA: Sage Publications, 2007), 101.

In its classic definition—"to see what is virtuous, suitable, and profitable"—prudence becomes the right action in a particular circumstance. It involves the whole person and includes the capacity to distinguish the concerns of self from those of others. A complex situation normally involves many moving parts—more precisely, people. Prudence becomes the virtue by which all the moving parts or concerns of everyone involved are moderated. Considering Kessler and Bailey's four features, prudence is therefore a blend of learning and experience in contradictory circumstances. In these moments, prudence involves using discretion, exercising caution, and conforming to the goal of "practical wisdom." Practical wisdom asks the question, "What should be done concerning this situation?" Within the parameters of this question, prudence is concerned with operating with good judgment, weighing all the possibilities, considering the consequences of one's actions, thinking before one acts, and using common sense. Therefore, prudent conduct cannot be rushed or hurried. In order to develop prudence, one must practice it.

If we reflect and meditate on our own experiences, and learn from them, these experiences tell us when and how we handled situations well or poorly. By personal reflection and evaluation, the capacity for prudent conduct is enhanced. These experiences, as we learn, enable us to "grade our own papers" concerning this virtue. The determination to be a prudent leader becomes a product of looking in the mirror.

Courage

> You gain strength, courage, and confidence by every experience by which you really stop to look fear in the face. You are able to say to yourself, I lived through this horror. I can take the next thing that comes along. You must do the thing that you think that you cannot do.
>
> —Eleanor Roosevelt

Courage requires internal endurance and fortitude. It is through endurance that leaders maintain the integrity of their consciences, especially in times of trial, and, to some degree, it is developed through life experiences. Melanie Greenberg said that courage is "an attribute of good character that makes a person worthy of respect."[19]

Greenberg stated further that there are different types of courage, ranging from physical strength and endurance to mental stamina and innovation. As a psychologist, Greenberg also added several attributes of courage that are particularly relevant to this session:[20]

1. Feeling fear, yet choosing to act
2. Following your heart
3. Persevering in the face of adversity
4. Standing up for what is right
5. Expanding your horizons—letting go of the familiar
6. Facing suffering with dignity or faith[21]

Greenberg's position relates to Havard's stance in the sense that courage is a virtue that can be practiced and made habitual. It is an attribute often present and active in a person's life. Courage sometimes reveals itself in crisis and uncertainty.

Courage is evident in the life of Cincinnati Bengals football player Devon Still and his daughter, Leah, who, as of this writing, is fighting for her life. In June 2014, then-five-year-old Leah was diagnosed with neuroblastoma, a rare form of pediatric cancer. "To watch my daughter fight for her life, that's a strength that I never knew existed."[22] When her father told Leah that she had cancer, she didn't ask what would happen if she didn't win the battle, but she agreed to fight all the same. Four days later, Leah started her first

---

[19] Melanie Greenberg, "The Six Attributes of Courage," Psychology Today. com, accessed October 25, 2014, http://www.psychologytoday.com/blog/the-mindful-self-express/201208/the-six-attributes-courage.

[20] Ibid.

[21] Ibid.

[22] Accessed July 18, 2015, http://ftw.usatoday.com/2014/11/devon-still-leah-still.

round of chemotherapy.[23] Although Leah has never met psychologist Melanie Greenberg, several attributes of courage from Greenberg's perspective are seen in Leah's fight for life. "Feeling Fear, yet choosing to act, following her heart, persevering in the face of adversity, and facing suffering with dignity or faith."

Leah's courage has made her a national inspirational example of courage. Unknown to Devon, the Bengals football team agreed that all sales of his number 75 jersey would be donated to the Cincinnati Children's Hospital to support pediatric cancer research. The Bengals organization never anticipated the astounding sales of the jersey.

Initially, the team ordered one thousand jerseys to be made available for purchase, but during Leah's six weeks of chemotherapy, close to fifteen thousand jerseys were sold, raising more than $1 million.[24]

Leah's life is an example of the virtue of courage that has made a difference. Leah Still's fight for life contains one or more of Melanie Greenberg's attributes of courage. This example suggests to leaders that courage is the ability to overcome fear, no matter what they may confront.

> I learned that courage is not the absence of fear, but the triumph over it. The brave person is not one who does not feel afraid, but one who conquers that fear.
> —Nelson Mandela

Self-Control (Temperance)

> I no longer teach the management of people at work …
> I'm teaching, above all, how to manage oneself.
> —Peter Drucker

---

[23] "#StillStrong: Devon and Leah Still's Journey from Cancer Diagnosis to Now," ESPN, accessed July 18, 2015, http://espn.go.com/espnw/news-commentary/article/13245405/devon-leah-journey-cancer-diagnosis-now.
[24] Ibid.

Self-control or temperance has a direct influence on how a leader's behavior and conduct is reflected in daily assignments and responsibilities in any setting. Temperance is a component of the emotional self or emotions (passions) that we all possess. Passion is defined as any powerful, compelling emotion or feeling. Plato considered the body to be the habitation of the soul; human passions are the chains that enslave it. From Plato's perspective, human freedom meant liberation from our passions.[25]

Yet when we consider our emotions, they are as much an expression of our humanity as the reality of our existence. To deny our emotions is to deny our existence. Still, it is vital that our emotions or passions are controlled and not allowed unrestrained expression. We need only to think about the consequences of intemperance to understand why leaders need self-control. The person who lacks self-control is capable of surrendering to the pursuit of power, profit, or pleasure. Such a person neither takes into account the common good nor offers respect to the dignity of others within the organization.[26] In addition, the lack of temperance or self-control undermines trust, which is the glue that holds everything together. If a team member is angered when contradicted or envious or jealous when others are promoted or otherwise recognized, other team members eventually will lose confidence in that person.[27] Intemperate behavior and lack of self-control will sabotage bonds of organizational cohesiveness.

Linda Kavelin, Dan Popov, and John Kavelin, in their book *The Family Virtues Guide*, stated, "Self-discipline means choosing to do what you feel is the right thing to do." It is bringing order and efficiency into your life and to those around you. These authors stated further, "When you are self-disciplined, you create and bring structure into your life."[28] This suggests that a pattern of self-control

---

[25] Ibid, 85.

[26] Ibid, 87.

[27] Ibid, 84.

[28] Linda Kavelin, Dan Popov, and John Kavelin, *The Family Virtues Guide: Simple Ways to Bring Out the Best in Our Children and Ourselves* (New York: Penguin Group, 1997), 233.

or temperance is created, and leaders are committed to following that pattern.

Of vital importance to self-control is that before leaders can expect to lead anyone else successfully, they must first lead and control their own selves. In so doing, the self-controlled or temperate leader sets an example worth emulating.

Justice

The *Merriam Webster's dictionary* defines the *just* person as one that is honest, conscientious, and honorable. Having or showing a strict regard for what is morally right.[29] Justice—giving others what they deserve or are due—takes practice. It also takes prudence, the first of the cardinal virtues. Justice flows directly from prudence. Prudence tells us the right thing to do in a particular circumstance. Prudence gives us the truth and shows us the way, and we act. Traditionally, justice is often broken into three broad categories, each of which demonstrates how we interact with others, based on our understanding of the following:

Commutative justice: This category explains the relationship between individuals within a given community.

Distributive justice: This explains the relationship of the community as a whole to individuals (e.g., fair wages and the distribution of resources).

Social justice: Living justly means acting or behaving justly that includes the idea of fairness for all members of society. Knowing the right thing to do (prudence) means little if the right action isn't taken.

---

[29] "Just," Merriam Webster's Dictionary, accessed September 27, 2022. www.merriam-webster.com.

Actions—or more specifically, *right actions*—are what justice is all about. Right actions are simply just actions and respect for all. Leaders are individuals, but they cannot be concerned only about themselves. Purposeful relationships and interaction with the community are beneficial to both. Just leaders view every person in their community as a human being who deserves dignity and respect.[30]

Justice is related intimately to the virtues of truthfulness and charity. Truthfulness requires courage—the courage to stand for moral truth, even if it means opposing the popular ideals or sentiments of others.[31] Truth is truth, regardless of others' opinions. Truth resides somewhere between what we think and how things actually are. Truth reminds us that a leader requires humility to recognize that there are still some things that we do not know. Truth stands as an ally to justice to remind us that it is never a matter of *who* is right; it is always a matter of *what* is right.

> And ye shall know the truth, and the truth shall make you free.
>
> —John 8:32

A just leader respects and honors the dignity of others, thereby creating a bridge of mutual respect that further solidifies unity in that particular community or organization. Just leaders understand that life is a gift from God and that everyone they lead should be treated fairly, equitably, and with dignity.

---

[30] Havard, *Virtuous Leadership*, 98.
[31] Ibid, 102.

PART II

THE AUTHENTIC LEADER AND CHARACTER DEVELOPMENT

Authenticity requires vulnerability, transparency, and integrity.

—Janet Louis Stephenson

To be authentic means ""representing one's true nature or beliefs; true to oneself or to the person identified."[32] Authenticity arises when a leader has the intention and determination to be genuine. Authentic leaders accept their strengths *and* weaknesses. They are accountable. They are connected to their values and desires and act deliberately in ways that are consistent with those qualities. The authentic leader majors in character development because authenticity demands it.

Heraclitus, a philosopher of the late sixth century, stated, "Character is destiny."

Walter Nicgorski, in his book *The Moral Crisis*, wrote,

> Strong personal courage should manifest itself in service to organizations and communities and courage in public life. The moral crisis of our time means more and more people lack the liberating

[32] https://business.tutsplus.com/tutorials/what-does-it-mean-to-be-authentic--cms-40517. Accessed September 27, 2022.

self-mastery that allows them to commit and serve with an independence and integrity befitting a free people.[33]

In the July/August 2009 issue of *Armed Forces Journal*, Lieutenant Colonel Donald Drechsler and Colonel Charles Allen (Ret.) wrote an article titled, "Why Senior Military Leaders Fail," in which they noted,

> In the first decade of the 21st century, the U.S. military observed the firings or resignations of the Chief of Staff of the Air Force, secretaries of the Army and the Air Force, plus several general officers, including the Commander of U.S. Central Command and most recently, the senior American commander in Afghanistan.[34]

Some of these leaders were fired, and others were asked to resign. The question that the authors' posed was why these intelligent and otherwise extremely successful senior leaders lost their jobs.

After decades of operating at senior levels of leadership, there is always the potential for and reality of the failure of character somewhere in the equation.

Max De Pree, the former CEO of Herman Miller, a company that produces office furniture and home furnishings, once said, "The first task of a leader is to help define reality."[35] The reality is that responsibility and accountability for a leader's actions accompany

[33] Walter Nicgorski, "The Moral Crisis: Lessons from the Founding," *The World and I* (September 1987): 7.
[34] "Why Senior Leaders Fail," *Armed Forces Journal* (July2009), http://armedforcesjournal.com/why-senior-military-leaders-fail/
[35] Rosenstein, Bruce. "How Max De Pree's Career Exemplifies Drucker's Art Of Leadership." Accessed September 30, 2022. https://www.managementmattersnetwork.com/notable-quotable/columns/how-max-de-prees-career-exemplifies-druckers-art

the position; this becomes a matter of character, and *character always matters.*

Warren Bennis, an American scholar and organizational consultant said that the ancient Greek translation of character means "to engrave, and its related noun means mark or a distinctive quality." Character is who we are, essentially, and our character is evolving continuously. It does not matter which position of leadership we hold; leadership is our character, and our character becomes our leadership. One cannot exist without the other. This portion of the session suggests that the evolution of character may be assisted by the use of the acronym RESUME.

- **R**esolute
- **E**mpathize
- **S**acrifice
- **U**nshackle
- **M**odel
- **E**ducate

To *resume* means to continue or begin again after a pause or interruption. The character-based leader understands that multiple responsibilities will consume his or her time and efforts daily. Distractions can sometimes pull the leader away from what is truly important. Benjamin Franklin stated, "Dost thou love life? Then do not squander time, for that's the stuff life is made of." A character-based leader guards his or her time and places great value on those matters that relate to the organization's mission.

There will always be those who will attempt to squander or waste your time. This is the place where the character-based leader must RESUME.

Resolute

The resolute leader charts a determined course of action. This type of leader possesses uncommon discipline, unwavering values, and strength developed through adversity; he or she is a passionate advocate of the future. The resolute leader recognizes that to succeed is the only course of action, and he or she is highly determined and persistent in doing so. These leaders are good problem-solvers and have a propensity to hold individuals accountable. They have high standards for themselves and others. They're often able to identify potential weaknesses in plans and have the courage to speak their minds.[36]

Empathize

To empathize is to experience the feelings of others vicariously. Empathy requires the willing, intentional, thoughtful, and honest practice of participating in another's feelings or ideas. Good leaders lead people, but great leaders empathize with people as they lead. When leaders walk with others, they create the opportunity to serve others' needs. To empathize with others is to serve them. In serving others, the authentic and empathetic leader develops a reputation as one who cares.

Sacrifice

Sacrifice involves devotion to a cause that includes the reality of loss. It is a disadvantage personally but is a gain for others relationally. Sacrifice involves selfless service. The authentic leader serves "self, less." There is no question that one must care for oneself. This is the place of self-leadership. Before leaders can lead others, they must

---

[36] Kristeen Bullwinkle, "Resolute Leaders (and Everything Disc)," DiscProfiles. com, accessed April 24, 2015, http://www.discprofiles.com/blog/2014/01/resolute-leaders-everything-disc.

learn to lead the self. A sacrificial leader always must pay a price. Development of the attribute of sacrifice requires maintaining a balance between sacrificing and replenishing. Those leaders who do not take time to replenish themselves through rest and reflection are subject to the dangers of overcommitment. When an authentic leader develops the reputation of one who is willing to sacrifice for others, it has a powerful, positive effect on those they lead. Sacrificial leaders produce sacrificial followers; self-serving leaders produce self-serving followers.

Unshackle

To unshackle oneself is the act of becoming free from restrictions or restraints. These restrictions or restraints can include fear of failure, fear of criticism, or simply a lack of confidence in self. Dennis Whaley once said, "Our limitations and success will be based, most often, on our own expectations for ourselves. What the mind dwells upon, the body acts upon." Many of our limitations are self-imposed because we compare ourselves to others. No two people are the same, and therefore, no two leaders are the same.

To compare ourselves to anyone else is to deny our unique natures. Authentic, unshackled leaders recognize talents and skills as gifts to the organization to which they belong. Gifts are always appreciated by those who receive them. Consequently, an unshackled leader consciously helps break the shackles of others.

Unshackled, authentic leaders do not walk in arrogance; they walk in the reality of healthy confidence in self that is balanced by humility.

Model

To be a model simply means to be an example who others can emulate. A model recognizes the fact that no matter where you may be as a leader, someone always is watching you. Someone once said,

"Character is what you do in the dark." I would add that character also is what you do in the light. The model leader recognizes that the next generation of leaders will sometimes seek to emulate modeled conduct and behavior. To be a model leader is to display a work ethic that affects the culture of the organization. Productive team members will model the behavior of their leaders when positive results are noted and appreciated. Therefore, it is crucial to understand that the model leader is always on duty. This certainly includes organizational responsibilities, but it also includes responsibilities at home and in social settings. A model leader shows team members how to do something and guides them through the process of imitating the behavior modeled. It is not a matter of cloning (we are all different); it is a matter of owning the principles that others can look to as an example of a model leader.

Educate

Education can be understood to mean knowledge acquired by an individual after studying particular subject matters or experiencing life lessons that provide an understanding of something. Education requires instruction of some sort from an individual or composed literature. The most common forms of education result from years of schooling that incorporates studies of a variety of subjects. Character-based, authentic leaders educate others about the values, principles, standards, and the "personality" of the organization to which they belong. The values, principles, and standards create a persona, and the persona demonstrates the mission of the organization.

In a hospital environment, the persona that is created relates to health and wellness. In an automobile factory, the persona created is the manufacture of vehicles. This is what we do; this is who we are as an organization. As an educator, the character-based leader focuses on creating and maintaining a positive organizational personality. Negative influences that can cause confusion or disruption are neither accepted nor tolerated. The character-based leader focuses on inculcating values and standards that create a positive persona for the organization.

This, in turn, further creates the persona of an organization that is positive and cares enough to train and educate its team members as a long-term investment. Bennis said earlier in this session, "Character is who we essentially are and our character is continuously evolving." RESUME has been offered as a way to continue to evolve in character development. To resume is to restart, as needed.

As new members are added to our leadership teams, we will need to rehearse the standards of the organization to which we belong. Character development always matters. It matters for a junior as well as a senior leader. Because character development is a part of the leadership journey, there are times when we will have to resume the preceding process. There is simply too much to lose if we don't lead with character.

PART III

WHY SHOULD WE CARE ABOUT CHARACTER AND VIRTUE?

It's not a matter of who's right. It's what's right.

—Nate Holcomb

There are those who believe that great leaders are born and not made, that they have innate leadership abilities. Havard, however, argued that leaders are not born in this sense but are *trained*.

Not everyone will be a Medal of Honor recipient or win a Nobel Prize. Everyone, however, can be "trained to grow in virtue, therefore, increasing strength of character."[37]

On September 8, 2014, former presidents Bill Clinton and George W. Bush unveiled a new presidential leadership program. The initiative is the product of collaboration among the presidential centers of Clinton, Bush, George H. W. Bush, and Lyndon Johnson. The goal of this initiative is character-building. The program involves approximately one hundred hours of case studies and approaches to leadership theory that draw from examples from recent presidents. The intent is that the participants will develop leadership skills that address the challenges and opportunities presented in the twenty-first century, with the goal of having an influence in their communities.

The program is designed further to bring together a select group of leaders who share a desire to solve complex challenges and create

[37] Havard, *Virtuous Leadership*, xiv.

positive change.[38] This initiative is indeed encouraging. The question that remains, however, is if the Presidential Leadership Scholars program would have affected the students and teachers at Columbine High School in Columbine, Colorado, where, on April 20, 1999, two senior students, Eric Harris and Dylan Klebold, murdered twelve students and one teacher.[39] Will the Presidential Leadership initiative influence young men who are like Adam Lanza? On December 14, 2012, Adam appeared at Sandy Hook Elementary School in Newtown, Connecticut, and killed twenty students, ages six and seven, and six adults. Prior to the shootings at Sandy Hook, Adam also shot and killed his mother.[40]

According to Everytown.org, since the December 2012 shooting in Newtown, there have been at least *128 school shootings* in America—an average of nearly one a week. Everytown is an organization of more than three million mayors, mothers, police officers, teachers, survivors, and gun owners who have come together in an effort to make their communities safer.[41]

Although the Presidential Leadership initiative is a tremendous program, the idea of virtue development in our school systems may be of even greater importance to our country. The characters and futures of our children are shaped and molded during early childhood. What would happen if the US Department of Education implemented an early childhood education initiative to develop virtue?

What would happen if our social studies or history curricula emphasized the ne cessity of virtue—*prudence, justice, courage,* and *temperance*—as the foundation of character development? Would a virtue-development program have made a difference in the life of former Minneapolis police officer Derek Chauvin? Chauvin was convicted of murdering George Floyd on Monday, May 25, 2020.

---

[38] https://www.presidentialleadershipscholars.org/about/. Accessed September 30, 2022.
[39] History.com Editors, "Columbine Shooting," History, accessed July 28, 2015, http://www.history.com/topics/columbine-high-school-shootings.
[40] https://www.britannica.com/event/Sandy-Hook-Elementary-School-shooting. Accessed September 30, 2022.
[41] Everytown, accessed July 28, 2015, http://everytown.org/who-we-are.

The evidence reports that Chauvin held his knee on or around the neck of a handcuffed and prone Floyd for more than nine minutes, as two other officers restrained Mr. Floyd.[42]

Would a virtue-development program have made a difference in the lives of the insurrectionists who stormed our nation's Capitol on January 6, 2021? According to an ABC News Go article, "Five people died during or after the attack, including four protesters and one police officer, and approximately 140 officers suffered injuries."[43] I don't believe that any character-based, value-centered leader and citizen could have ever imagined such an assault on American democracy.

Modern medicine has given us the ability to take x-rays of broken bones and the ability to use an MRI to discover cancer cells in our bodies and blood clots in our brains, but we have yet to determine how a person thinks. A portion of how every American citizen should think is noted in our Declaration of Independence:

> We hold these truths to be self-evident, that all men are created equal, that they are endowed by their Creator with certain unalienable Rights, that among these are Life, Liberty, and the pursuit of Happiness.[44]

As American citizens, our Constitution grants us certain inalienable, irrevocable rights, but I do not have the right to infringe upon another person's rights to life, liberty, and happiness. January 6, 2021, contained no elements of life or happiness at all.

---

[42] Dan Mangan, "Former Minneapolis cop Derek Chauvin set to plead guilty in federal civil rights case for George Floyd," CNBC, Dec. 13, 2021, https://www.cnbc.com/2021/12/13/derek-chauvin-will-plead-guilty-in-george-floyd-killing-federal-case.html.

[43] Olivia Rubin, Alexander Mallin, and Will Steakin, "By the numbers: How the Jan. 6 investigation is shaping up 1 year later," ABC News, Jan. 4, 2022, https://abcnews.go.com/US/numbers-jan-investigation-shaping-year/story?id=82057743.

[44] "Declaration of Independence: A Necessary Break," Academy 4SC, Accessed July 30, 2015, https://academy4sc.org/video/declaration-of-independence-a-necessary-break.

Another way to capture this idea of caring about character and virtue is simply this: "Do unto others as you would have them do unto you." This portion of the session is subtitled, "Why should we care about character and virtue?" We should care about character and virtue as leaders because many others do not. It is one thing to talk about character and virtues in public, but it is an entirely different matter for one to live a life of character and virtue. Would a (character) virtue-development program have made a difference in the life of Derek Chauvin? Would a (character) virtue-development program have made a difference in the lives of the insurrectionists on January 6, 2021?

We are too late to answer that question for them, but we can make an effort to answer it for others—particularly for those we lead. Individually, I may not be able to change or influence the entire world, but as a leader with virtue and character, I am determined to make the best possible effort every day for those I lead.

As each day transitions into the next in the very busy lives we all lead, we sometimes forget what has happened in the past. Spanish-born American philosopher George Santayana said, "Those who do not remember the past are condemned to repeat it."[45] Virtue and character development are not just for our schools or early childhood education. To live a virtuous life carries the connotation of a life of solid moral conduct, particularly moral excellence. Virtues are qualities of the mind, the will, and the heart that instill strength of character and stability of personality.

Plato's four main virtues of prudence, justice, courage, and temperance (self-control)—the "cardinal virtues"—are those upon which all other virtues hinge. As Santayana reminded us, lessons of the past ought to prepare us for the future.

As it is in any profession or occupation, these traits must be practiced and made habits in order for us to become competent as virtuous people or leaders. A virtuous style of leadership is realized when this is accomplished, and it makes a difference in the organizational world to which we belong.

---

[45] https://en.wikiquote.org/wiki/George_Santayana, Accessed November 11, 2014..

PART IV

ASCENDING TO A VIRTUOUS MINDSET

You don't climb a mountain without a team, you don't climb a mountain without being fit, you don't climb a mountain without being prepared, and you don't climb a mountain without balancing the risks and rewards. And you never climb a mountain by accident—it has to be intentional.

—Mark Udall

Perhaps the greatest challenge in climbing a mountain is simply to get started. If you are going to climb, rise, or ascend to a virtuous mindset, the challenge is starting the climb. As stated earlier in this session, virtue is the essence of our character and when, as leaders, we keep the practice of virtues at the forefront of our daily decision-making, this further inculcates the conduct of moral excellence.

A mindset may be defined as ideas and attitudes that are habitual or characteristics, and they determine how individuals will interpret and respond to various situations in the workplace and life. The climb or the ascension required to achieve a virtuous mindset must be practiced and intentional in order to be accomplished. In this session, the highway that one must take to ascend to a habitual, virtuous mindset is composed of the lanes of effectiveness, efficiency, expectancy, enthusiasm, and encouragement, all of which establish excellence as a virtuous mindset.

Effectiveness as a Virtue

> Never mistake motion for action.
>
> —Ernest Hemingway

To be effective is to "successfully produce the desired or intended result or goal." The origin of our English word *effective* traces back to the Latin word *effectivus* and its root word *efficere*, meaning to "work out or accomplish."[46] Effective leadership occurs when every member works in unison. Effective teams have learned the basic ingredients to success. The effective leader simply needs to remind the team about what has made it successful and that those are the things that it must continue to do.

What effective leaders and teams do consistently is illustrated by 3 Rs:

- Rehearse
- Reach
- Regular

Effective leaders and teams *rehearse* policies, guidelines, and goals consistently to provide team members with a well-rounded vision of team goals, including how they will be achieved and how they will be measured. Setting clear and direct goals and guidelines prepares the team for the proper evaluation of performance. Effective leaders and teams also *reach* for a consistent understanding of their individual roles and responsibilities, thus preparing their team members for success. Periodic evaluations of team members' strengths and weaknesses provide opportunities to address concerns through training and mentoring programs. This also includes capitalizing on the diversity of the talents within the team.

Every member brings different skills and capabilities to the table. Learn what those talents are and use them. Continual assessment

---

[46] "Effective," Vocabulary.com, accessed April 20, 2015, http://www.vocabulary. com/dictionary/effective.

and *regular* feedback for the team and each individual member will help everyone stay on track. Address overall team issues in meetings and provide a concrete plan to correct any issues while maintaining the mindset of, "We are a championship team, and together there is nothing that we cannot accomplish."

Efficiency as a Virtue

> A particular shot or way of moving the ball can be a player's personal signature, but efficiency of performance is what wins the game for the team.
> —Pat Riley

If a person or a procedure is efficient, the job will be done well, and no time will be wasted. If you are *effective*, you do a job properly; if you are *efficient*, you do it quickly and easily, performing in the best possible manner with the least time and effort.

Efficiency as a virtue also means having the required knowledge and skills and being competent and capable.[47] If efficiency is lacking, a leader first must identify why some team members are more efficient than others. What motivates one team member may not necessarily motivate another. However, the reason that someone is a member of the team is to do his or her part. When members of the team fail to perform their share of the tasks, other members must not only accomplish their own tasks but must assume someone else's responsibility.

Does a team member's performance and behavior suggest that there may be personal problems of which you may not be aware? Is the attitude of the team member consistent with organizational aims and goals? After questions like these and others have been addressed and resolved, if the team member consistently lacks motivation, and efficiency continues to wane, the efficient leader must think of the

[47] "Efficient," The Free Dictionary, accessed April 20, 2015, http://www.thefreedictionary.com/efficient.

overall good of the team. Could the lack of efficiency be because the team member no longer desires to be part of the organization? Efficient leaders evaluate and review all possible outcomes, both for the organization and for the individual, and help team members make the right decisions, both personally and organizationally.

It is also necessary to evaluate potential "time thieves" or distractions. A time thief can be a lack of focus on the assignment or daydreaming. A time thief can also result from a lack of proper rest. The organization has hired the team member for a particular number of hours per day. If that person does not come to work rested properly, functional efficiency will decline. The efficient leader can recognize and address appropriately the time thieves that arise among the team that decrease efficiency.

Another strategy for efficiency is to encourage taking mental breaks, whether getting a cup of coffee, getting up from the computer, taking a walk outside, or simply turning off the telephone ringer. The efficient leader sets up his or her team for success and creates the optimum work environment. For some team members, rewards play an important role in job satisfaction and productivity. Rewarding team members who complete outstanding work by applauding their efforts in internal newsletters or giving them plaques may increase personal efficiency, which, in turn, may motivate others in the organization and increase overall efficiency.

Efficient leaders and team members use the most of each minute of the day, giving their full attention to the most important tasks first. Efficiency not only improves productivity but also creates a sense of accomplishment and satisfaction.

Expectancy as a Virtue

> If you hold positive expectancy in the front of your
> mind, it will appear in the palm of your hand.
>
> —Linda Chandler

Expectancy is the "act or the state of thinking, believing or hoping that something positive will happen."[48] Yale University professor Victor Vroom is credited with what he called the expectancy theory of motivation, which is based on the three components of "valence, expectancy, and instrumentality." *Valence* refers to the capacity to affect another. It is the level of confidence a team member has that a desirable outcome will result from his or her actions. *Expectancy* is the outcome a team member or employee anticipates in response to his or her actions or behavior.

Instrumentality refers to the qualifications and abilities a team member has to perform the work necessary to produce a desirable outcome. The theory suggests that an individual's perceived view of an outcome will determine his or her level of motivation. The theory assumes further that the choices an individual makes reflects the person's belief that, "If I accomplish this, I will get that." The theory also suggests that people engage in behaviors that have pleasant outcomes and avoid behaviors that have unpleasant outcomes.[49]

This also means that the expectant leader is one who operates with optimism and closes the door on pessimism. Clearly, it can be difficult to remain optimistic during certain times in your life—for example, when the challenges of the economy make it difficult to take care of your family.

The expectant leader, however, creates hope when and where hopelessness arises. The expectant leader imparts to team members or employees that it is necessary to believe in themselves, work hard, do the right thing, be dependable and reliable, and have an expectancy that something positive will happen for them in the organization.

When valence, expectancy, and valuing team members become part of the operating standards of the organization, the questions of "What's in it for me?" or "What about me?" will never be asked

---

[48] "Expectancy," The Free Dictionary, accessed April 20, 2015, http://www.thefreedictionary.com/expectancy..

[49] https://courses.lumenlearning.com/wmintrobusiness/chapter/reading-expectancy-theory/. "Lumen Introduction to Business," accessed September 30, 2022

because they will have been answered and proven daily by expectant organizational leadership.

What potentially transpires is the "ripple effect." The ripple effect is the continuing and spreading results of an event or action. The ripple effect then becomes embedded in the character and culture of the organization as the norm, which stimulates team members to expect the best.

Enthusiasm as a Virtue

> I found that the men and women who got to the top were those who did the jobs they had in hand, with everything they had of hard work, energy, and enthusiasm.
>
> —Harry S. Truman

Enthusiasm may be defined as "an intense and eager enjoyment, interest, or approval." The word comes from the Greek *enthous*, which means "possessed by a god, or inspired."[50] Enthusiasm is contagious. When you work with enthusiastic people, you can't help but be enthusiastic yourself.

Think of people with whom you have worked. Usually, those who show enthusiasm are those with whom you enjoy working, while those who have little enthusiasm usually bring you down. This is true not just at work but also in your personal life. Enthusiasm by itself can do only so much, but when enthusiasm is coupled with respect and collaboration with others on the team, mountains can be moved.

The enthusiastic leader does not portray a false or phony enthusiasm. The enthusiastic leader is the model of a person of value and merit, a person to emulate. The enthusiastic leader openly does what others may be reluctant to do. Whatever the task may be, he or

---

[50] "Enthusiasm," Lexico, accessed April 20, 2015, www.oxforddictionaries.com/us/definition/american_english/enthusiasm.

she undertakes it with a positive attitude. For example, if faced with a problem, the enthusiastic leader does not talk about the problem; the enthusiastic leader becomes the solution to the problem. The problem is seen as a starting point to move forward, rather than as a reason to complain or allow negativity to infect the team or the organization. The enthusiastic leader engages everyone that the problem affects. This means that the leader asks for assistance in finding a solution because the enthusiastic leader states clearly that everyone's input is important and will not be ignored. Thus, the enthusiasm to resolve the issue is the main focus of the conversation.

This enthusiastic demonstration of leading others forward demonstrates positive responses. Examples like these of an enthusiastic leader become pillars of a positive organization, where enthusiastic leaders create enthusiastic followers.

Encouragement as a Virtue

> I consider my ability to arouse enthusiasm among men the greatest asset I possess. The way to develop the best that is in a man is by appreciation and encouragement.
>
> —Charles M. Schwab

Encouragement is the act of imparting hope, courage, confidence, and resolution to inspire, persuade, or urge. All of us need encouragement. Encouragement can have a powerful effect on coworkers and bosses. It has been said, "One word of encouragement in the times of failure is worth more than one hour of praise or compliment after success." Colleagues and senior leaders face challenging situations, and they fail or make mistakes daily. Everyone needs encouragement, from the most senior to the most junior leader in the organization.

Encouragement helps us deal and cope with fear, doubt, uncertainty, and disappointment. Each organization desperately needs leaders who encourage its members for giving their best efforts in the midst of failure or rejection.

The encouraging leader acknowledges and accepts that each individual needs encouragement occasionally, so encouragement must be given organizationally. The encouraging leader truly cares about team members. Even if people display a hard outward demeanor (even if they handle the negative emotions and reactions that accompany a mistake or failure calmly), the encouraging leader discerns and responds accordingly. When leaders impart confidence, hope, resolution, and inspiration to others, an intrinsic belief is established. This newly developed mindset is able to overcome discouragement because courage has been added. *Courage* is the quality of mind or spirit that enables a person to face difficulty through inner strength. The idiom "take heart" means to receive courage. The encouraging leader imparts courage in times of discouragement by:

- Reassuring team members after a setback, failure, or disappointment that he or she is with them.
- Giving purposeful expressions of appreciation for the contributions each team member makes.
- Exerting a positive influence on team members' lives whenever the opportunity presents itself. This fosters the mindset among employees and team members that leadership cares.
- Deliberately looking for ways to encourage others, verbally or in writing.
- Helping others on the team believe in themselves by pointing out positive characteristics and how those attributes can lead to success in their lives.

Excellence as a Virtue

Excellence is the result of caring more than others think is Wise, Risking more than others think is Safe,

> Dreaming more than others think is Practical, and
> Expecting more than others think is possible.
>
> —Ronnie Oldham

One definition of excellence is the "quality of being outstanding, distinguished, or superior." The ancient Greeks defined excellence with the term *arête*. In its basic sense, *arête* means "excellence of any kind." The term may also mean "moral virtue."

In its earliest appearance in Greece, the idea of excellence was connected to the fulfillment of purpose or function—the act of living up to one's potential. Arête is associated frequently with bravery but more often with effectiveness. The man or woman of arête is a person of the highest effectiveness, one who uses all his or her faculties—strength, bravery, and wit—to achieve real results.[51] Beyond the definition, excellence is a set of established leader beliefs, ways of thinking, and focusing, as well as discipline. Vince Lombardi once said, "Perfection is not attainable, but if we chase perfection we can catch excellence."

Excellence entails setting a high standard for yourself and focusing on becoming better each day. It is an inward focus that produces outward results. To "catch excellence," as Coach Lombardi said, we must deem excellence to be quintessential to the pursuit. The status quo is unacceptable when and where greater possibilities may be achieved. From this perspective, excellence as a virtue is the insatiable quest to set the highest standards for oneself and other members of the team.

Excellence, therefore, becomes a way of life, and nothing less will suffice. A pragmatic approach to catching excellence or pursuing excellence as a way of life is to EAT, which means that leaders continue to develop **e**motional maturity, **a**daptability, and **t**eachability. If we agree that leadership is a journey and not a destination, everybody has to eat along the way!

---

[51] Simoes, Jussara, https://swa.proz.com/personal-glossaries/entry/1594640-arete-aret%C3%AA, accessed September 30, 2022.

Emotional Maturity as a Virtue

To be mature is to have knowledge and experience about the way self and the organization function. Emotional maturity does not mean that a leader is forbidden to express emotions; it means that an excellent leader does not allow emotions to control behavior. An emotionally mature leader has experienced the full range of emotions. As a result, emotionally mature leaders understand the consequences of their emotions and the necessity to keep them under control.

The emotionally mature leader remains calm and is unmoved by the eruption of emotions from others that can create a problem that threatens the unity and harmony of the team and organization.

The emotionally mature leader is a part of the solution, not the problem. Team members learn quickly to distinguish between those who are emotionally mature and those who are not. As team members experience emotional maturity from their leaders, it creates confidence within the organization. Emotionally mature leaders also strive to develop a balance between confidence and self-awareness in order to trust their own decisions and to accept the criticism and correction necessary if they make incorrect choices.

The emotionally mature leader is one who continues to train to achieve excellence, both in self and in the organization, because excellence is the standard of life and leadership.

Adaptability as a Virtue

To be adaptable is to "readily adjust oneself to changing or different conditions." Adaptability means understanding that not everything will go your way. The ability to adapt, especially when it involves other people, is a sign of emotional maturity.

Developing a sense of flexibility and adaptability requires patience. There is a saying: "Blessed are the flexible (adaptable), for they will not be bent out of shape." Adaptability enables the excellent leader to make calm and informed decisions. Adaptability also includes the ability to remain self-motivated, even when things go wrong. Because no one is perfect, there is no perfect organization. When things progress unexpectedly, the emotionally mature leader adapts and moves forward, regardless of the obstacles. This is not the occasion for blame. The emotionally mature leader seeks to fix what has gone awry, to adapt, and to strategize progress. This reflects the recognition that mistakes will be made simply because we all are human. The signature of motivation and adaptability will be written on the hearts of those who follow; in turn, they will write their own chapters of motivation and adaptability by the example of their leaders.

Teachability as a Virtue

One who is teachable is one who may be instructed. Life is a constant classroom. After the journey through elementary, junior high, high school, college, and postgraduate school, life and leadership say, "There is still more to learn."

After the accomplishment of any and all academic endeavors from within, a leader who is truly teachable says, "I need to learn more in pursuit of excellence." Teachability is the desire to listen, learn, and apply. It is the willingness to learn, unlearn, and relearn. A teachable attitude welcomes teachable moments.

A teachable moment is the ability to learn from any place, person, circumstance, or situation. Valuable leadership principles can be acquired by being observant and asking questions, such as:

- Am I open to other people's ideas?
- Do I listen more than I talk?
- Am I open to changing my opinion based on new information?
- Do I readily admit when I am wrong?
- Am I open to doing things in a way I haven't before?

- Am I willing to ask for directions or help?
- Do I act defensive when criticized, or do I listen openly to the truth?

The preceding questions and others like them point to the necessity of periodic self-evaluation. This is a part of the process of Ethnos Leadership: a self-evaluating, self-reflective way to discover, develop, and disciple (mentor) to make a difference.

Some may say that their daily schedules keep them very busy. Everyone is busy now. Everything that a leader engages in is important, but not everything is urgent. There is an often-quoted saying: "Poor planning on your part does not constitute an emergency on my part." To be teachable also includes being taught to manage time. The excellent leader is not managed by time but rather manages it. To do so, one must invest, rather than spend time. An investment of time always provides a tangible return on the investment. To spend time may lead to lost time that can never be recouped.

Harvey Mackay once said, "Time is free, but it's priceless. You can't own it, but you can use it. You can't keep it, but you can spend it. Once you've lost it you can never get it back."

Excellence as a virtue reveals itself in the language you use, the questions you ask, the people with whom you surround yourself, and how you interact with others. Abraham Lincoln said, "Be excellent to each other," while Aristotle stated, "We are what we repeatedly do. Excellence, therefore, is not an act, but a habit." An excellent leader is one who is in pursuit of or living a life that excels. The pursuit is practiced consistently and persistently, and in so doing, character and virtue are strengthened.

A Final Thought Concerning Character and Virtue

The *Titanic*, the ship reported to be unsinkable, sank at 2:20 a.m. on April 15, 1912, when it struck an iceberg in the North Atlantic Ocean.[52] The iceberg was certainly a factor in the tragic loss of life that night. However, what was later proven to be a major contributor to the sinking of the ship was the "lack of character [strength] of the ship's hull."[53]

The builders of the *Titanic* believed that they had created an unsinkable ship. Scientists who have studied samples of the hull retrieved from the wreck found that the ship was built with substandard steel. In addition to a shortage of steel plates for the hull, there was a shortage of steel rivets and expert riveters to piece the hull together. The company was forced to use lower-grade wrought-iron rivets, which impact tests showed were more brittle.[54] Along with many other factors in the sinking of the ship that night, one thing noted was that the integrity or strength of the ship's hull was insufficient to withstand an iceberg.

It does not matter what your status or position in life may be. Whether you are a professional athlete, a stay-at-home mom or dad, one who serves proudly in our military forces, a minister, a physician, or a nurse, your strength of character will eventually be tested. Suggested in this session is that the habitual practice of the virtues of prudence, justice, courage, and temperance will strengthen and enhance one's character. When tested or confronted by the unexpected circumstances in life, the question remains: is a leader's character—the practice of a virtuous life—strong enough to avoid sinking?

Havard's point earlier was that "virtue practiced habitually

---

[52] History.com Editors, "Titanic Sinks," History, accessed July 7, 2015, http://www.history.com/this-day-in-history/titanic-sinks.

[53] https://www.history.com/news/why-did-the-titanic-sink. "Why did the Titanic Sink?" accessed September 30, 2022.

[54] Ibid.

enhances professionalism." This same principle is true for a responsible citizen in a civilized society.

Professional football players or actors in Hollywood are much more often in public view than you or I, but the point is clear. Society expects more from high-profile athletes and celebrities. Does money blind some to their moral responsibility as citizens? Is it the status of being famous or a celebrity?

To practice one's profession without the practice of sound moral virtues that strengthen character leads inevitably to the true nature of a person. Saint Augustine once stated,

> Humility is the foundation of all the other virtues hence, in the soul in which this virtue does not exist there cannot be any other virtue except in mere appearance.

At the end of each day, considering the research and examples cited, the development of character and virtue is a choice that includes humility. Humility is not weakness but rather meekness, which is strength under control. The choices that we make eventually will produce the sum of what our lives have been or will become.

Summation of Character and Virtue: The Foundation of Authentic Leadership

As mentioned earlier, the National Leadership Index 2010 showed that America's confidence in its leaders was significantly below average for the third year in a row. Nonetheless, quiet, unassuming leaders all around us—whom we know as wives and husbands, sons and daughters, coworkers and neighbors, police officers and firefighters, emergency service personnel, and teachers—are great men and women making a historical difference in society because of their influence. This foundational attribute is accounted for by the values of character and virtue that a person possesses individually, which affects all communities, collectively.

One dictionary definition says that influence is "the capacity or power of persons or things to be a compelling force that produces effects on the actions, and behavior of others." Of particular note in this definition is the phrase *compelling force*.

The word *compelling* means "having a powerful and irresistible effect," while the word *force* suggests "strength or power exerted upon an object or power and the ability to convince." Goethe said, "Behavior is a mirror in which everyone displays his own image."[55] In so doing, the process of self-discovery continues uninterrupted daily. Most, if not all, of us look into a mirror daily. The question that we must ask ourselves continually as we look into the mirror is, "What about me as a leader needs to change?" Change is constant and inevitable.

This portion of the book has suggested that the driving factor in the crisis and necessity for change in leadership is the ability to impart virtues that are habitual and that strengthen a leader's character. Drucker stated, "It is character through which leadership is exercised," while Havard suggested that it is the habitual practice of the set of classical human virtues—prudence, courage, self-control and justice—that make up the content of a person's character.[56]

---

[55] Quinn, Thomas. https://thomquinn.com/behavior-mirror-self/. Accessed September 30, 2022.

[56] Havard, *Virtuous Leadership*, xiv.

This session also focused on the need to be authentic. To be authentic means, "Not false or copied; genuine or real. Having its origin supported by unquestionable evidence, authenticated, verified, accurate and reliable."[57]

Authenticity starts when a leader intends to be genuine. Authentic leaders accept their strengths and weaknesses. They are accountable. They are connected to their values and desires, and they act deliberately in ways that are consistent with those qualities. It does not matter what position of leadership one may hold; leadership is personified by character, and character becomes the quality of one's leadership.

Also suggested was that the continued evolution of character development as leaders includes RESUME. Leaders must be "resolute, empathetic, sacrificial, unshackled modelers and educators."

On the journey to becoming an Ethnos leader (a leader of character), a virtuous mindset must be practiced and intentional. There are occasions that demand ascension to obtain a virtuous mindset that further undergirds excellence.

As discussed in this session, the suggested highway to a habitual, virtuous mindset includes the lanes of effectiveness, efficiency, expectancy, enthusiasm, and encouragement that assist the leader in developing excellence and a virtuous mindset. As with the *Titanic*, a ship that was built to be unsinkable, so it is with leaders at every level. There will always be circumstances or situations where the "hull of our ships" (our characters) will be tested. The question remains: Is my character strong enough to withstand today's test? For the Ethnos leader who wishes to make a difference, the habitual practice of the virtues designed to strengthen character is a constant ally, both now and in the future.

---

[57] "Authenticity," Lexico, accessed April 24, 2015, http://www.oxforddictionaries.com/definition/english/authentic..

Questions for Reflection

1. If the National Study of Leadership is correct concerning a leadership crisis, what steps from this session can you initiate or implement that will help to minimize the reality of this perspective from your position as a leader in the organization or company to which you belong?

2. If both personal and organizational change is constant and inevitable, what principles from this session can you employ to ensure change has a positive, rather than a negative, effect on your team?

3. Virtue development or education is not currently a part of the rules and procedures of the organization to which you belong. With your influence as a leader, how could you persuade your supervisors or senior leaders of the value of virtues in strengthening character?

4. Considering your organizational culture, how would you answer objections to virtue education, both from those who follow you and those whom you follow?

5. Explain the influence of a leader who behaves authentically in espousing the principles and values of the organization to which he or she belongs.

Quotes of Principled Leaders

Champions do not become champions when they win the event, but in the hours, weeks, months, and years they spend preparing for it. The victorious performance itself is merely the demonstration of their championship character.

—T. Alan Armstrong

I admire men of character, and I judge character not by how men deal with their superiors, but mostly how they deal with their subordinates, and that, to me, is where you find out what the character of a man is.

—General Norman Schwarzkopf

I hope I shall always possess firmness and virtue enough to maintain what I consider the most enviable of all titles, the character of an honest man.

—George Washington

SESSION II

IDEAL MODELS AND PRACTICES OF LEADERSHIP

Foundation

Leadership is one of the world's oldest occupations. Stories have been told through the generations about leaders' competencies, ambitions, and shortcomings. This history of leadership includes discussions of leaders' rights, privileges, duties, and obligations. The study of leadership can be traced back to the Old and New Testaments of the Bible, the Greek and Latin classics, numerous Egyptian rulers, Plato, Sun Tzu, Confucius, and many others.[58]

In approximately AD 100, Plutarch tried to illustrate the similarities between fifty Greek and Roman leaders. Latin authors, such as Caesar, Cicero, and Seneca, to name just a few, wrote extensively on the subject of leadership and administration. Their influence was considerable on medieval and Renaissance leaders, who looked to the classics for guidance. Napoleon listed 115 qualities that are essential for military leaders.[59] Leadership, however, has only

---

[58] Bernard Bass, *Bass and Stogdill's Handbook of Leadership: Theory, Research, and Managerial Applications* (New York: the Free Press, 1990), 3.
[59] Ibid., 5–6.

become the focus of contemporary academic studies in the past sixty years, particularly in the last two decades.[60]

From its infancy, the study of history has been the study of what leaders did and why. Discussions of specific ideologies or theories of effective leadership formed during the twentieth century. Several different theories can be applied to leadership; thus, there are no right or wrong theories but many different perspectives.

In its continual search for improvement and for the way to create the most effective leaders, the United States Army also began to reevaluate the discussion of leader development.

Today, the US Army defines leadership as "influencing people by providing purpose, direction, and motivation, while operating to accomplish the mission and improve the organization."[61]

As an example, the *trait theory of leadership* suggests that leaders have certain traits that make them good leaders. This theory focuses on the leaders' values and beliefs, personality, need for achievement or acceptance, orientation to power, gender, confidence, and their mental, physical, and emotional attributes. Early leadership trait theory assumed that people were born with specific traits, some of which were aligned with strong leadership. People with the "right" traits would become the best leaders.[62] In contrast, the *behavioral theory of leadership* states that leaders are made, rather than born. From this perspective, successful leadership is based on definable, learnable behavior.

Behavioral theories do not seek inborn traits; they seek evidence of leadership through action. The implication is that leadership capabilities can be learned.[63]

---

[60] "Leadership studies," Wikipedia, accessed April 8, 2015, http://en.wikipedia.org/wiki/Leadership_studies#History_of_Leadership_As_A_Field_of_Study.
[61] Sewell, Gerald. "Emotional Intelligence and The Army Leadership Requirements Model."https://usacac.army.mil/sites/default/files/documents/cace/DCL/DCL_SewellEngNovDec09, accessed September 30, 2022.
[62] Ibid.
[63] https://www.wgu.edu/blog/leadership-theories-styles2004.html#close. "Leadership Theories and Styles," accessed September 30, 2022

In the 1970s and 1980s, researchers such as James MacGregor Burns and Bernard M. Bass developed *transformational leadership theory*, which is based on the assumption that people will follow a leader who inspires them. Another leadership model, *transactional leadership*, assumes that people are motivated intrinsically strictly by reward and punishment. This style generally does not appeal to the values, morals, or other inherent characteristics of most people. The transactional leader focuses on tasks, provides very clear direction, and oversees productivity in detail. When a subordinate this theory includes a penalty or punishment.[64] According to the *contingency theory of leadership*, the leader's ability to lead is contingent upon various situational factors, including his or her preferred style, the capabilities and behaviors of followers, and various other situational factors.

Contingency theories are a class of behavioral theories that contend that no single aspect of leading supersedes another and that an effective leadership style in some situations may not be successful in others. An outcome of this theory is that effective leaders at one place and time may become unsuccessful, either when transplanted to another situation or when the factors around them change.[65] The situational leadership model supports the idea that influencing and leading people is not compartmentalized into one method or best practice. This style of leadership is consistent with the task versus people orientation.

This leadership theory holds that a leader's most appropriate action or behavior depends on the situation and the followers. The motivation and abilities of team members tasked to follow leadership will affect the leader's decisions in each situation.

There are four styles of leadership in this model:

---

[64] Cherry, Kendra." How A Transactional Leadership Style Works." https://www.verywellmind.com/what-is-transactional-leadership-2795317, accessed September 30, 2022.

[65] "Contingency Theory," Changing Minds, accessed April 9, 2015, http://changingminds.org/disciplines/leadership/theories/contingency_theory.htm.

- Delegating
- Supporting
- Coaching
- Directing

The theory assumes that each of these leadership styles can be effective, depending on the developmental levels of the leader and the team. In this theory, how one leads isn't a question merely of skills and abilities; leadership also depends heavily upon the attitudes embraced by the leader.[66]

The first goal of this session is to provide a brief history of leadership. The second goal is to review current models and practices of leadership that have proven successful for consideration of practical application. The study of leadership as a discipline includes a vast number of definitions, theories, styles, functions, and competencies. Ethnos Leadership is grounded in discovering, developing, "disciple-ing" (mentoring), and making a difference in other people's lives. It is a self-evaluating, self-reflective process of continual leader development for the practicing leader.

In defining *practice*, the *Oxford English Dictionary* says that it is "the actual application or use of an idea, belief, or method, as opposed to theories relating to it. It is the carrying out or exercise of a profession, especially that of a doctor or lawyer."[67]

As doctors or lawyers are said to "practice" their professions, so it is with today's leaders. The goal of Ethnos Leadership is that individual leaders discover and determine to develop, disciple (mentor), and make a difference, personally and organizationally.

It is not the intent of this session to determine which is the best or most effective method, style, or theory of leadership. The intent is to suggest that when certain practices and principles of leadership are applied, they will add value to today's practicing leader.

---

[66] https://asana.com/resources/situational-leadership, accessed September 30, 2022.

[67] "Practice," *Oxford English Dictionary*, accessed April 9, 2015, http://www.oxforddictionaries.com/definition/english/practice.

PART I

SELECTING BEST PRACTICES
OF LEADERSHIP

Considering best practices of leadership is really a matter of personal preference. Some may even disagree with the concept of "best practices" because of the question of *who* decides what constitutes best practices. The best answer to that question is that the individual decides. In every profession, if individuals desire to excel, they must practice and sharpen their skills in their trade or profession.

There are certainly many more best practices in leadership, but the point in this portion of the session is that throughout your leadership journey, you should find the *best* practices that work for you and put those practices to work in your leadership.

The discussion below focuses on seven suggested best practices to consider.

1. **Develop a personal and organizational cadence or rhythm.** While in basic training in 1976, I discovered that our drill sergeants had mastered the art of calling cadence. A cadence is rhythmic in nature. Whether on a ten- or twelve-mile road march with a sixty-pound rucksack or on a five-mile run, the cadence caller's task was to motivate and encourage. With the right cadence caller, we felt that we could run or march all day! Developing a personal and organizational cadence carries the idea of movement and motivation to a

particular destination. Whatever the task or assignment that needs to be achieved, we are better together when no one is left behind. At some point, everyone has experienced the feeling of being drained, mentally or emotionally, or being overwhelmed by the many responsibilities of adult life— among them, family challenges (sickness or illness), career issues (passed over for promotion), or financial anxiety.

Developing a personal and organizational cadence includes using the right words at the right time to provide a rhythm that connects with people. This is the responsibility of organizational leadership to keep the team moving towards the desired goal or objective. Movement and motivation are critical elements of success. Our drill sergeants mastered the art of calling cadence, which always gave us the strength to keep moving when we were frustrated or exhausted by the demands of the training cycle.

Someone once said, "Strength does not come from what you can do. It comes from overcoming the things you once thought that you could not do." You are stronger than you know. There is nothing that cannot be overcome.

> Whenever you find yourself doubting how far you can go, remember how far you have come. Everything you have faced, all the battles you have won, just remember everything that you have overcome.
>
> —N. R. Walker

2. **Focus on outcomes, not simply activity.** Activity is not always equal to productivity. An outcome follows as the result of a particular action. The nature of this practice simply says that goals must be set and a strategy implemented to achieve the desired outcomes. This includes a periodic measurement of accomplishment of the established goals and outcomes. It is possible to see a lot of movement or activity in the workplace

without clear evidence that tasks are being accomplished. Remind the team that you lead to focus on questions such as, "What's the goal?" or "What's our desired outcome?" and "How do we get there?" Organizational collaboration always brings clarity and possible solutions to the problem.

A laser is able to cut with great precision because it is focused. Establishing a laser-like focus on given goals and desired outcomes carries the organization to a higher level of productivity. It challenges employees or team members to commit 110 percent to organizational outcomes, and it answers the "What's in it for me?" question that arises inevitably. This question is answered by creating an incentivized environment where team members want to do more than the norm. An incentive motivates someone to do something, or it is something of personal value.

Sometimes these incentives are intrinsic, such as receiving satisfaction from work or the feeling of making a difference in the world. Extrinsic incentives include cash rewards or bonuses, but for some, it's not always about money. External incentives can include such things as peer recognition and increased social status, authority, or power.

Technology mogul Steve Jobs once said,

> The only way to do great work is to love what you do. If you have not found it yet, keep looking. Don't settle. As with all matters of the heart, you will know when you find it.[68]

Focusing on the outcomes is a part of loving what you do. This is the benchmark of an organization that focuses on outcomes and that is not distracted by unproductive activity. Telling every team member, "Well done," when appropriate and deserved, sometimes may be all the incentive needed

---

[68] https://news.stanford.edu/2005/06/12/youve-got-find-love-jobs-says/, accessed September 30, 2022

to maintain focus on organizational goals and achieve the desired results.

3. **Practice "people work," not paperwork**. Borrowing from Jobs' philosophy:

> Technology is nothing. What's important is that you have a faith in people, that they're basically good and smart, and if you give them tools, they'll do wonderful things.[69]

Despite all of the advantages of modern technology, the most valuable component of an organization or company will always be people. It is important that there is a shift in how we think about the structure of an organization. The new bottom line is that people must be the top line—put people over profit. Equally as important, however, is that without profit, there will be no need for the people because you will not have the money to pay their salaries! Every company is in business to make money, and if it does not, it will not be in business for long.

Paperwork represents all of the necessary business components of the organization's daily operation, from acquiring new customers and retaining existing ones, to acquiring new equipment, making deposits and withdrawals at the bank, and taking care of building maintenance—the list goes on. *People work* represents what makes people work. Some people work in order to provide the basic essentials—food, clothing, and shelter—for themselves and their families and to attain their desired standard of living. What makes some people work *where* they work is synonymous with an old proverb that says, "If you find a job that you love, you will never work a day in your life," which meets more than Maslow's hierarchy of needs (physiological needs, safety,

---

[69] https://internetpoem.com/steve-jobs/quotes/technology-is-nothing-what-s-important-is-that-you-32372/, accessed September 30, 2022.

love, esteem, and growth or self-actualization).[70] Yet there are a rare few in the workplace who rise above the basic essentials. For these few, where they work and why they work there includes an internal sense of satisfaction, significance, security, and safety.

Satisfaction involves the idea of doing something that is both gratifying and rewarding. *Significance* indicates making a difference, something that will matter because of the investment of our time and talents in certain organizational projects. *Security* involves a sense of loyalty that the organization provides to its team members. Security also carries the idea of *safety*, which means that where we work, we are accepted, appreciated, recognized, and respected. We must never lose sight of the importance of accomplishing the paperwork, which is represented by the necessary daily business operations. With this, we must always remember that the new bottom line is that people must be the top line. When people's work is first, the paperwork will be accomplished with greater expediency and efficiency.

4. **You cannot lead everyone in the same way because everyone is not the same.** We learned in elementary school that there are only twenty-six letters in the English alphabet. *The Economist* states on its website that the average adult has a vocabulary that ranges between 20,000 and 35,000 words. By the age of four, children already know 5,000 words, and by the age of eight, they know 10,000 words.[71] It is remarkable that all of the words in our vocabularies, whatever their length, originate from the same twenty-six letters. We were not given more letters as we and our vocabularies grew. Each word in our vocabularies has its own significance to us in the process of communicating and exchanging information. From this

---

[70] Saul McLeod, "Maslow's Hierarchy of Needs," Simply Psychology, accessed July 20, 2015, http://www.simplypsychology.org/maslow.

[71] R. L. G. "Lexical facts," *The Economist* (May 29, 2013), http://www.economist.com/blogs/johnson/2013/05/vocabulary-size.

perspective, practicing that each person is unique and distinct is a catalyst for learning. As members or employees, what we have in common is that, organizationally, our objectives ought to be the same. Yet we each are as diverse as the vocabulary that we possess. Just as our vocabularies grow, so must our understanding of each team member or employee.

Practicing leaders take time to understand the backgrounds and values of their employees. From this position of relationship in which people are actually engaged, it is possible to exert a greater influence on employee attitudes and motivation. This leads to the development of stronger connections among team members for the benefit of all involved. Because a large portion of an employee's life is spent at work, take the time to know what's personally important to your employees. Ask about the well-being of their families. This shows a level of concern and care that further develops bonds of credence and veracity.

Our vocabulary grew from a foundation of only twenty-six letters. Similarly, what we all have in common are the objectives of the organization to which we belong. It is important to remember that no one is the same, and therefore, no one can be led in the same way. As it is with our vocabularies, so it is with practicing and understanding each employee or team member individually. Growth occurs, and through this growth, the capacity to influence and lead diverse people with authenticity becomes an organizational reality.

5.   **Ask the right questions**. The right questions always begin with, "What can I do to help you succeed?" When team members believe that their supervisor has a genuine desire for them to succeed, it creates a level of trust. When leaders are not true to the words they speak, there is a greater potential that their personal trust account with their employees will become bankrupt. When people succeed personally, the organization succeeds exponentially. Upon hiring an employee, every

organization expects that the new team member is capable and qualified for the job for an agreed-upon salary. The exchange is simple and fair: do the job, and you will be paid for it. This practice of asking the right questions is related to the health of the person and the organization. By asking the right questions—which begins with "What can I do to help you succeed?"—the platform is built for a relationship between employer and employee that is open, healthy, and communicative. The health of an organization provides the context for everything that happens there. Leadership must have an open-door policy that is both credible and believable so that people who have been employed by the organization for a longer time will say openly to new team members, "If you have a problem, go see the boss. You can be assured that he [or she] will listen." To say that a leader has an open-door policy when the door truly is never open destroys credibility, and the organization suffers. It is not only that the boss listens that leads to growth but that the boss responds to help the team members succeed by patient, persistent training in their jobs.

Colin Powell, one of the most influential leaders of our time, said,

> The day soldiers stop bringing you their problems is the day you have stopped leading them. They have lost their confidence that you can help them or concluded that you do not care. Either case is a failure of leadership.[72]

Responsible employees want to do their jobs and do them well; being responsible also means knowing when a matter is beyond their capabilities. A functional open door permits

---

[72] JD Meier, "Great Lessons Learned from Colin Powell," Sources of Insight, accessed July 20, 2015, http://sourcesofinsight.com/lessons-learned-from-colin-powell.

employees to go see the boss because the leader asked the right question: "What can I do to help you succeed?"

6. **Realize that we live in a real, not an ideal, world**. It is important never to forget that we do not live in a perfect world. Neither people nor organizational systems are perfect, but structures, standards, and rules are in place to ensure that we do not devolve into chaos and confusion. On occasion, no matter how much effort employees may have invested in accomplishing a task or assignment, there is the potential of falling short of standards. This practice focuses on the proverb: "Blessed are the flexible, for they shall not be bent out of shape."

While serving in the army, there was a principle that every leader adopted: adapt and overcome. A contingency plan was always in place. Adapt to what has occurred and move on to accomplish the assignment or mission. Someone once said, "If you fail to plan, you plan to fail." What I would add to this precept is that whatever backup plan that you have, have a backup for the backup! The point with a backup for your backup is to adapt and overcome the obstacles and accomplish the assignment. It must be done!

7. **Celebrate like no one is watching.** Songwriters Susanna Clark and Richard Leigh wrote a very popular song in 1987 that included the lyrics, "Dance Like Nobody's Watching.".[73] This song summarizes best practices of leadership but also best practices for life; the necessity of celebration. To celebrate is to do something special or enjoyable, to honor or observe a notable occasion. It also means to commend or "have a ball." The philosophy of working hard and playing hard is one that every leader should possess. When we were children, we played hard because it seemed like that was all there was to do! The stress of everyday life without a change of pace can

---

[73] "Dance Like Nobody's Watching," Quote Investigator, accessed July 19, 2015, http://quoteinvestigator.com/2014/02/02/dance

be just as crippling to employees as when the equipment in a factory shuts down.

An article in *Business Insider* stated that the average person spends 90,000 hours at work during his or her lifetime.[74] To celebrate is to enjoy life, not simply endure it. Everyone experiences hardships and difficulties that can sometimes be debilitating. The practicing leader learns to celebrate those they have the privilege to lead. This is called *deliberate celebration.* Celebrating significant moments with employees is making the decision to regain from our childhood our ability to "play" as often as is appropriate in the workplace. I hope that you dance (celebrate) with those you lead like nobody is watching because when you dance with your team, they will know that whatever is significant in their lives is also significant in your life as their leader.

---

[74] Rachel Premack, "17 Seriously Disturbing Facts about Your Job," Insider, accessed July 19, 2015, http://www.businessinsider.com/disturbing-facts-about-your-job-2011.

PART II

MORE PRACTICES FOR THE PRACTICING LEADER

Don't practice until you get it right. Practice until you can't get it wrong.

—George W. Loomis

Leadership development never has been and never will be "one size fits all." Included in this portion of the session are models and examples of best practices of leadership because of their practical and relevant approach to leader development. It has often been said that the largest room in the world is the room for improvement.

I read an article about the practice habits of basketball legend Larry Bird, which said that Bird shot five hundred free throws before going to school every morning. As a twelve-time NBA All-Star, the league's Most Valuable Player in three consecutive years, and a member of a team that won three NBA championships, Bird understood the value of practice.[75] He knew that to win or succeed at any profession, practice, practice, and more practice is the key!

It will always be necessary for leaders at every level to continue to improve and expand their leadership skills, understanding, and influence for the health and wellness of their organizations. Healthy

---

[75] https://en.wikipedia.org/wiki/Larry_Bird, accessed September 30, 2022.

leaders are growing leaders. Healthy, practicing, growing leaders become CEOs who are contemplative, enabling, and obligated.

The Contemplative Leader

A growing leader is a contemplative leader. Contemplation, as the ally of anticipation, brings excitement and enthusiasm about the possibilities for the future of the organization. Developing the ability to contemplate requires letting go of the past and focusing on the future. Contemplation is deep, reflective thought— mediation on and imagination of a desired future state. For many, the disappointments of the past hinder the perspectives of the future.

Charles Kettering, an American engineer, once said, "My interest is in the future because I am going to spend the rest of my life there." As we live one day at a time, trusting and believing not only in self but also in the organization to which we belong, we anticipate and contemplate a better future. When Walt Disney was fired from a local newspaper at age twenty-two because, according to the editor, he lacked creativity, Disney had to contemplate a better future for himself.[76] The values of determination, creativity, and contemplation of practical strategies become the catalysts that produce momentum in the present for a higher-quality future. In 2012, the Walt Disney Company held assets of $74.9 billion.[77]

Disney developed the ability and competency to let go of the failures and unsuccessful business ventures of the past and to contemplate and ultimately create a better future for himself, his family, and the organization that we now know as Walt Disney Company.

---

[76] Amethyst Tate, "Celebs Who Went from Failures to Success Stories," CBS News, accessed April 16, 2015, http://www.cbsnews.com/pictures/celebs-who-went-from-failures-to-success-stories/15.

[77] "Total Assets of the Walt Disney Company," Statista, accessed April 16, 2015, http://www.statista.com/statistics/193136/total-assets-of-the-walt-disney-company-since-2006/.

The Enabling Leader

A practicing leader is also an enabling leader. Enabling others is the behavior of a confident leader. When employees are enabled, it prevents them from being hindered in their job performances. If the task is to dig a twelve-by-twelve–foot ditch, the assignment could be accomplished by using a spoon or a shovel. The enabling leader provides the shovel and not the spoon for the assignment. The enabling leader does not hinder team members by poor communication, and he or she provides clear expectations about assignments.

The enabling leader is not threatened by the potential of junior leaders in the organization. An enabling leader shares his or her experience and knowledge about how to accomplish the organization's goals and mission with all team members. An enabling leader also is a mentor. Francis Bacon once said, "Knowledge is power," while Goethe stated, "Knowing is not enough; we must apply. Willing is not enough; we must do."

The point is that the enabling leader shares the necessary knowledge that enables others to act. No leader has all the knowledge, and anyone who expects this to be true has missed the point of leadership development. A leader is expected to function and be responsible, and if an answer is unknown, the leader must demonstrate credibility and accountability to find the answer. This is the reason leaders occupy specific positions of leadership. Unless knowledge is applied, no influence manifests to the benefit of the person or the organization. From this perspective, the enabling leader becomes a mentor who is available at all times to share experience and knowledge. In this process, the enabling leader may identify strengths and weaknesses that can and must be addressed. It is at this point that the enabling leader institutes a process of purposeful investment to enhance success. When team members succeed, the organization succeeds.

The Obligated Leader

The obligated leader accepts the call of duty to facilitate progress and continuous improvement in trust and interdependence. To be obligated in this sense carries the meaning of "being morally bound to someone or something." The obligated leader is always ready to serve. In our world of heightened security at airports, locked homes and cars, and passwords and pass codes to protect information on computers, it is difficult for people to demonstrate or experience trust. Creating trust and interdependence between leaders and followers is consistent with what Helen Keller, a blind philanthropist once said: "Alone we can do so little; together we can do so much."[78] This type of trust goes beyond title or position in the organization and moves toward extraordinary relationship development. Opportunities to continue to build upon these extraordinary relationships are before us every day, and the obligated leader engages this dynamic purposely.

A good reputation spreads throughout the organization just as quickly as a bad one. An obligated leader creates a "trust account" by consistently proving trustworthiness; in this process, trust is forged. This is the motor of the obligated leader's personal leadership, and it drives the entire organizational system. It is a standard of operation agreed upon mutually by the leader and the team, not in the sense of a democratic vote but in the sense of "buying into" or believing in the concept.

Personal success and satisfaction, in essence, fuel the obligated leader. The more energy the leader generates, the more energy the team or organization has in a virtual, continuous cycle of reinforcement. It is the obligated leader's duty to reinforce a clear and persuasive story of purpose.

The obligated leader becomes the catalyst for change that provides energy to the team. Every organization has a paradigm or pattern for operation. My contention is that a healthy practicing leader becomes

---

[78] https://www.brainyquote.com/quotes/helen_keller_382259, accessed September 30, 2022.

a "CEO": contemplative, enabling, and obligated to practice and be effective in his or her efforts within the organization. With this, the practicing leader continues to ask, "How do I improve daily as a leader?" The pursuit and corresponding action should provide the answer to the question. If the answer is not satisfying, continue the daily pursuit.

Never be satisfied with today's successes because tomorrow will bring another challenge. This will involve risk-taking. Mistakes and perceived failure will challenge the CEO as a practicing leader, but failure is never final, as long as one learns and matures. The accomplishment of any and all organizational goals begins in collaboration.

PART III

COLLABORATION AND COMMUNITY AS PRACTICE

Collaboration and a sense of community (mutual respect) lead an organization to engage in extraordinary group efforts. Collaboration is simply working together. In this, leaders merge and leverage the abilities of others. They encourage others to feel strong, capable, and confident to take initiative and accept responsibility. If leaders want greater levels of trust and collaboration organizationally, they must demonstrate their trust *in* others before asking for trust *from* others.

To some extent, collaboration is self-disclosure. Letting others know what we stand for, what we value, what we want, what we hope for, and what we are willing (and not willing) to do entails disclosing information about ourselves, which does not occur without some personal risk. When a leader is willing to take risks of this nature, it also creates a willingness among team members to do the same. People are more inclined to take personal risks when organizational risk-taking has proven to be safe.

Collaboration also strengthens dedication and commitment. The collaborative leader strengthens and encourages team members to take ownership and responsibility for the organization's success by enhancing their competence and confidence in their own abilities. In contrast, people in the organization who feel powerless tend to develop petty and uncooperative attitudes. Although it may not be verbalized or discussed, when an individual perceives power or control over his or her personal destiny within the organization, personal effectiveness increases. By sharing power (collaboration) or giving power away, followers or team members develop greater competence and confidence, which benefits the entire organization because they are trusted to do so.

Community

In creating a spirit of community, the "common unity" breathes and breeds life into the organization. The values and the purpose to which the community connects further create a spirit of community. To breathe and breed life is not a common mindset in organizations.

A spirit of community, however, with the preceding mindset creates a strong and vibrant organizational culture that strengthens further commitment to the culture. Community fosters a sense of oneness and solidarity that promotes loyalty and devotion. It is inevitable that stressful and challenging times will arise within an organization.

The *Oxford English Dictionary* defines a community as "a group of people living in the same place or having particular characteristics in common." Community is made up of the words *commune* and *unity*. Commune means "a group of people living together who share possessions and responsibilities, or people who share common interests."[79] The Online Etymology Dictionary adds that unity is "the state of being one"; the state of being united or whole. Creating a spirit of community enables the organization and its team members to endure challenging times because of the concept of oneness—we take care of each other.

On many occasions in over twenty-seven years of military service, I knew after a deployment or a long field-training exercise that a story was about to begin when someone exclaimed, "And there we were!" It did not matter if it was a large or a small group,

---

[79] "Commune," Dictionary.com, accessed April 13, 2015, http://dictionary.reference.com/browse/commune.

everybody knew that a story was beginning. Normally, it related to the entire unit, an experience that everyone could recount. In telling the story, we were able to recall the good, sometimes the bad, and sometimes the downright ugly experiences of it all. Yet the greatest significance of the story was that we made it, and we made it together. Celebrating the values and victories of the organization includes public expressions of the accomplishments of team members. With a thank-you note, a smile, and public praise, the leader lets others know how much individual team members mean to the organization.

They make a point of telling others in the organization what each member of the team has achieved, and in doing so, they make others feel like heroes.

Another aspect of creating community is simply the example that leaders set. What is this example? It is the same thing that sustains the follower: the answer is love equals profit. In his book, *Love and Profit: The Art of Caring Leadership*, James Autry wrote,

> Creating a caring environment, a place in which people have friendships and deep personal connections and can grow personally, emotionally, psychologically, and spiritually, as well as financially and professionally, is an important platform for creating profit.[80]

In such a community, the organization will experience consistent profit, not loss.

The influence and power of love in our society and what it means have been distorted and abused to the point that few understand its true meaning. In the truest definition, love is the unconditional acceptance of another. No one is perfect, and all have flaws, but we are all better together because we have a common purpose in the organization to which we belong, and *we all* have the potential to encourage the hearts of others. By creating a spirit of community

---

[80] James Kouzes and Barry Posner, *Credibility: How Leaders Gain and Lose It—Why People Demand It* (San Francisco: Jossey Bass, 2011), 169.

among team members and by setting an example of love, an exceptional organizational atmosphere and environment is built, which becomes a model for other organizations (communities) to practice.

PART IV

THE PRACTICE OF BUILDING

The best principles of leadership are found in leadership that is active, practiced, and functionally operational. Principled leaders practice continually the principles of formation needed to create the desired organizational environment. Many may recall from the days of our childhood the ever-present building blocks that our parents gave us. Stacking the blocks one upon the other sometimes challenged us to see who could build the tallest tower of blocks without it falling over.

From this same viewpoint, the shaping or the path of organizational development is analogous to building blocks. To build a tower, the blocks have to be stacked one at a time. By no means is this an exhaustive list, but I offer here three significant arenas for the practice of building:

- Culture
- Communion
- Choices

Culture

The first block is culture. Culture may be defined as a particular set of characteristics, beliefs, thinking, and behaviors of a person or organization that provides a further sense of identity. Culture may also be defined as:

> All the ways of life including arts, beliefs and institutions of a population that are passed down from generation to generation. Culture has been called "the way of life for an entire society." As such, it includes codes of manners, dress, language, religion, rituals, art. norms of behavior, such as law and morality, and systems of belief.[81]

From this perspective, to be effective, culturally aware leaders must know where they come from and which values have made them who they are. They can connect the dots of their lives to the life of the organization to which they belong. Building an organizational culture purposefully is an ideal model of leadership because its focus is on team building. If teams are to work effectively, all employees must understand and embrace the culture of the particular group or business to which they belong.

Emotional maturity and authenticity and a strong character are essential if leadership is to be effective in a culture-driven organization. Culture contains life experiences by which the leader has been shaped. A culturally aware leader must be aligned closely with the culture of the organization and, in a broader sense, with the languages, nationalities, ages, and interests of its employees or team members.

This type of leader is thought of as a person devoted to a cause, in whom the values of the organization and team members are articulated explicitly, rather than implicitly. In this way, there is no confusion or ambiguity attached to the leader who practices cultural awareness. In addition, this kind of leader is seen to have a personal commitment to success that is obvious, is verbalized frequently, and often is imitated. The leader who practices cultural awareness and appreciates diversity demonstrates consistent passion and energy for the work to be done. The culture itself produces the drive and

---

[81] https://sphweb.bumc.bu.edu/otlt/mph-modules/PH/CulturalAwareness/CulturalAwareness2.html, accessed September 30, 2022

inspiration to accomplish the mission without central leadership because enough people believe in the cause of the organization's culture.[82]

Communion

In its Latin origin, *communion* is *communionem*, which means "fellowship, mutual participation, a sharing." As used by Saint Augustine, the word was derived from *com*—"with or together"—and *unus*—"oneness, or union." This part of the building process speaks to the aspect of faith in the equation of leadership. The argument for the existence of or faith in God is left to the philosophers and is not deliberated here. The point is that everyone has faith in something or someone. Faith can be defined as "a strong belief or trust in someone or something."

Communion, or the leader's personal relationship with God, is perhaps the most critical aspect of the building process and practice because it requires faith. Faith in God speaks to an encounter with the supernatural. From this perspective, people can have faith in a car or faith that sitting in a chair at Starbucks will support their weight. Yet this is not the kind of faith that transforms or influences change. Faith in God is the belief that God exists. The question arises, "Which God (god) are we talking about?" WorldPopulationsreview.com has compiled a list of "Major Religions of the world by country." The following is a list of religious populations by number of adherents and countries.[83]

- Christianity: 2.1 billion
- Islam: 1.5 billion
- Secular/nonreligious/agnostic/atheist: 1.1 billion

---

[82] Arkad Kuhlmann, "Culture-Driven Leadership," Ivey Business Journal, accessed April 14, 2015, http://iveybusinessjournal.com/publication/culture-driven-leadership.
[83] https://en.wikipedia.org/wiki/List_of_religious_populations, accessed September 30, 2022.

- Hinduism: 900 million
- Chinese traditional religion: 394 million
- Buddhism: 376 million
- Primal indigenous: 300 million
- African traditional and diasporic: 100 million
- Sikhism: 23 million
- Juche: 19 million
- Spiritism: 15 million
- Judaism: 14 million
- Baha'i: 7 million
- Jainism: 4.2 million
- Shinto: 4 million
- Cao Dai: 4 million
- Zoroastrianism: 2.6 million
- Tenrikyo: 2 million
- Neo-Paganism: 1 million
- Unitarian-Universalism: 800 thousand
- Rastafarianism: 600 thousand[84]

To be aware of team members' various religious and cultural beliefs is essential in establishing the kinds of relationships in the organization where respect for diversity and concern for all becomes the focus of activity in the workplace. It is well understood that our world is large and diverse, with varying viewpoints and religious beliefs. To a large extent, a leader's personal relationship with God will depend upon community and culture.

The key to this portion of the session is the word *personal*. To be clear, from the perspective of Ethnos Leadership, communion is a personal relationship with the Judeo-Christian heritage and the nature of the God of the Bible. In its original Greek translation, the word *communion* is *koinonia*, which means, "having in common, a partnership or fellowship." Paul, the New Testament apostle in the Bible, said to his disciple Timothy, "I know in whom I have

---

[84] Ibid.

believed ..." (2 Timothy 1:12). In 1 Timothy 6:12, Paul said to Timothy, "Fight the good fight of faith." These were both matters of Paul's heart toward Timothy and included the influence of faith and prayer in a person's life.

Prayer is a pillar of a leader's partnership with God. A partner does his or her part. The part of the believer is to have faith and believe that God's part is to be God.

In remarks broadcast from the White House as part of a February 7, 1954, American Legion program, President Dwight D. Eisenhower declared,

> As a former soldier, I am delighted that our veterans are sponsoring a movement to increase our awareness of God in our daily lives. In battle, they learned a great truth—that there are no atheists in the foxholes. They know that in time of test and trial, we instinctively turn to God for new courage ... Whatever our individual church, whatever our personal creed, our common faith in God is a common bond among us.[85]

Communion from this perspective is a leader's personal relationship with God, which is a matter of choice and a matter of the heart. This portion of the book suggests that as an ideal model and practice, faith in God is a prerequisite to building community through understanding the culture of one's team. Respecting and embracing diversity keeps leaders on the path of learning and growth. As the leader grows, a personal relationship (communion) with God and with others will continue to develop.

George Washington once said, "Every man ought to be protected in worshipping the Deity according to the dictates of his own

---

[85] "There Are No Atheists in Foxholes," Conservapedia, accessed April 13, 2015, http://www.conservapedia.com/There_Are_No_Atheists_In_Foxholes#cite_note-3.

conscience."[86] Communion is personal, and leaders must know in whom they believe.

Choices

It has been said that who we are today is a result of the choices that we made yesterday. In this sense, choices are what the leader does, commonly and consistently, through habit or routine. To a certain extent, this parallels the quote, "Character is what you do in the dark when nobody else is watching."

Daily choices embody personal conduct. According to HealthyBrain.org, the average person has approximately seventy thousand thoughts a day.[87]

In an article in the *Huffington Post*, Bruce Davis wrote:

> Of those 70,000 thoughts, this means we have between 35 and 48 thoughts per minute per person. The steady flow of thinking is a filter between our thoughts and feelings, our head and heart.[88]

Sarah Lambersky, in her research for the *Financial Post*, said,

> We produce up to 50,000 thoughts a day and 70% to 80% of those are negative. This translates into 40,000 negative thoughts a day that need managing and filtering.[89]

[86] "One Nation … Under God?" Sullivan-county.com, accessed April 14, 2015, http://www.sullivan-county.com/nf0/dispatch/fathers_quote2.htm..

[87] https://healthybrains.org/brain-facts/, accessed September 30, 2022.

[88] Bruce Davis, "There Are 50,000 Thoughts Standing Between You and Your Partner Every Day," HUFFPOST (May 23, 2013), http://www.huffingtonpost.com/bruce-davis-phd/healthy-relationships_b_3307916.html.

[89] Sarah Lambersky, "How to Manage Your 40,000 Negative Thoughts a Day and Keep Moving Forward," *Financial Post* (Oct. 16, 2013), http://business.financialpost.com/entrepreneur/three-techniques-to-manage-40000-negative-thoughts?__lsa=a51b-5b78.

As practicing leaders, to change the *outcome* of our futures, we must change consistently the *income* of our thinking about matters of daily choice or the commonplace. Negative circumstances or negative people possess a natural ability to destroy anything that resembles that which is positive. Negative thoughts can lead to negative choices, which may happen unexpectedly and without warning. What we choose to do with that which is perceived as negative will determine what happens next.

An experience with a rude team member or an arrogant, pretentious leader undoubtedly produces a negative thought. If, however, through consistent habit or routine, a leader has practiced to *respond* rather than *react* (it is not easy sometimes), that which has the potential to be a negative experience can be transformed into a positive one. The idea of responding and not reacting to the negative is a matter of the nature of one's character, which again is a matter of choice. To respond is to answer in words or with a particular action, which can be negative or positive. To react is to act in opposition to or against something. The practicing leader recognizes each situation for what it is and has developed the ability to defuse the situation, rather than allow it to explode. By not allowing a potentially negative situation to explode, the ideal practicing leader protects the team and organization from collateral damage. If left unchecked, negativity can spread to other team members and create a toxic organizational environment

As it is with conflict, the leader must make the choice to transcend the negative and obtain a clear perspective of the situation; then, the leader must determine or understand why a person is displaying such a negative attitude or disposition. Has the team member recently received troubling or disturbing news? Has the team member been challenged by another team member?

Over the last several years, the reality of bullying and cyber-bullying by and against our youth has received national attention. Although bullying may not be as overt among adults, the possibility and potential for it is present in the workplace as well. It has often been said that people who have been hurt will hurt other people. If a leader can determine where the pain resides, the potential to change a person's attitude from negative to positive can be determined as well. There is a prescription for the pain.

The responsible practicing leader knows each member of the team *personally* and practices knowing his or her employees daily. Daily choices, together with the consistent and persistent pursuit of development, not only *instruct* but *construct* the pattern by which one leads. Although I do not possess the skills of a tailor or seamstress, I do understand that you need a pattern to make a suit or dress. Before an automobile rolls off the assembly line, the designers follow a particular pattern. A leader's daily choices both instruct and construct the environment of influence.

Over forty years of leadership experience (instruction) and life lessons have taught me how to construct a day of my choosing. There always will be circumstances and situations beyond a leader's control, but the leader does have control over self. The very nature of one's character is what enables a person to choose what happens when confronted with circumstances beyond his or her control. In essence, whatever is revealed by the leader's responses or reactions to those circumstances pertains to life and leadership.

Whatever becomes part of a leader's daily habits has the potential to become a best or a worst practice of leadership. What does a responsible, aspiring leader do with fifty thousand to seventy thousand thoughts a day? If Sarah Lambersky is correct that 70–80 percent of those thoughts are negative, what does the practicing leader do? It is the leader's choice to decide what he or she will practice to overcome negative and potentially destructive attitudes and circumstances, both personally and organizationally. It is by choice or routine that accountability facilitates maturity. In this, I make the choice to trust somebody to help me walk in honesty and integrity.

Each leader and each team member is a work in progress. No one is perfect, and we all are better together. Through this process, maturation in life and leadership provides a greater understanding of what makes a great leader. To be a great leader, one must first be a great person; the cart should never go before the horse. Through this process, a great person inherits the traits and potential to become a great leader. Before they were military heroes, philanthropists, inventors, or sports or movie legends, they all had the potential to be great people, which, in turn, made them great leaders. Great leaders who began as great people will always make a difference in the world.

Summation: Ideal Models and Practices of Leadership

The primary objective of this session was to provide a general history and brief discussion of different styles, models, and theories of leadership. In addition, the goal was to look briefly at successful models of leadership for consideration in practical application. There has been and will continue to be much discussion about specific ideologies or theories of what it takes to be a leader. The study of leadership as a discipline is filled with a vast number of definitions, theories, styles, functions, and competencies. A theory provides background, insight, and solid understanding. Yet for practical leadership development, theory must move from the abstract to the concrete.

No theory is necessarily better than another, but there are many different perspectives. There always will be a need to expand our perspectives of leadership because of the constancy of change. The practice of leadership has many similarities across various theories and models. A good leader may draw from several models and theories or may decide to continue the leadership journey based on other models and theories not discussed in this session. Some may conclude that one model or style is better than another. Others may say that empirical data are needed to support a particular position or viewpoint of leadership. The point is whether one can say, as is the title of Colin Powell's book, *It Worked for Me in Life and Leadership.*

Just as all of us have different tastes in music and food, most of what we choose is due to personal preference. Ethnos Leadership is designed for leaders to continue to discover, develop, and disciple (mentor) to make a difference across nations and in people's lives. As a principle-centered leadership process, the aim of Ethnos Leadership is to recognize and discover what works for each leader personally and to allow it to work.

Questions for Reflection

1. Consider the leadership theory with which you identify most. How do you apply it for daily application with those you lead?
2. In creating the ideal model of leadership for your organization, what elements from this session (or other sources) would you include?
3. What is the function of faith in leadership?
4. What strategy would you use to help those you lead to understand the importance of constructing a day of their choosing?
5. What steps could you take when you notice that the building blocks of culture, communion, and choices appear to be teetering in your organization?

Quotes of Principled Leaders

There are three types of leaders: those who make things happen, those who watch things happen, and those who wonder what happened.

—Nicholas Murray Butler

Leadership cannot really be taught. It can only be learned.

—Harold S. Geneen

Leadership is unlocking people's potential to become better.

—Senator Bill Bradley

Today we are faced with the preeminent fact that, if civilization is to survive, we must cultivate the science of human relationships——the ability of all peoples, of all kinds, to live together, in the same world, at peace.

—Franklin D. Roosevelt

You don't develop courage and character by being happy in your relationships every day. You develop it by surviving difficult times and challenging adversity.

—Epicurus

SESSION III

PROVEN PRINCIPLES OF CHARACTER DEVELOPMENT

Foundation

The United States Military Academy at West Point has been educating, training, and inspiring leaders of character for the US Army and for America for more than two hundred years. West Point is designed to help its cadets choose a direction in life that puts service to the nation first and allows graduates to be standard-bearers for their generation and the generations that follow. Everything that cadets experience is focused on developing them as leaders of character who will serve as officers when they are commissioned as second lieutenants in the US Army. As these new leaders begin their military careers, they become leaders of soldiers, and each new promotion brings additional responsibility, as well as increased opportunity.[90]

The mission statement of the United States Military Academy (USMA) is:

> To educate, train, and inspire the Corps of Cadets so that each graduate is a commissioned leader of character committed to the values of '*Duty, Honor,*

---

[90] "A Brief History of West Point," United States Military Academy, West Point, accessed December 7, 2014, www.usma.edu/wphistory.

> *Country'* and prepared for a career of professional
> excellence and service to the Nation as an officer in
> the United States Army.[91] (italics added)

The West Point experience, a four-year process, involves more than just academics. The West Point Leader Development System (WPLDS) is a holistic developmental system with the overarching goal of graduating commissioned officers who are warriors, leaders of character, servants of the nation, and members of the profession of arms, prepared for intellectual, ethical, social, and physical demands across a broad spectrum of challenges. This system is the framework employed at West Point to develop cadets' competence and character simultaneously. The academic, military, and physical programs at West Point are the main driving agents of this development.

Throughout a cadet's forty-seven-month experience, these three programs (academic, military, and physical) are structured purposely to provide cadets with the foundation for continued growth and development. Through this approach,

> A cadet's identity is transformed from a personal self-
> interest perspective to one more oriented toward
> a self-authored standard or code of conduct that
> provides the basis for informed, responsible, self-
> directed decision making.[92]

The six specific domains in these three programs, through which cadets are developed, are intellectual, military, physical, social, moral-ethical, and human spirit. The human spirit, the moral, ethical, and social domains focus on establishing a cadets' identity. This is designed to bolster character and expand their perspectives. The intellectual, military, and physical domains focus on developing in cadets the knowledge, skills, and competencies critical for establishing

---

[91] *Building Capacity to Lead* (New York: United States Military Academy, West Point, 2009), vi.

[92] Ibid., 6.

the professional foundation of officership (the practice of being an army officer) and to foster continued growth as a strategic thinker and leader.[93]

All three programs promote and provide opportunities that urge cadet or leader growth in each domain. As cadets develop intellectually, militarily, physically, socially, and spiritually through successful completion of activities within the academic, military, and physical programs, as well as cadet activities and intercollegiate athletics, they also develop morally and ethically. Throughout the West Point experience, the ability to develop morally and ethically is accomplished by embedding the consideration of principles and adherence to moral principles, army values, and the professional army ethic. The ultimate goal of the WPLDS is to assist cadets in the development of the concept of what it means to be a commissioned leader of character.[94]

Notable graduates from West Point include two American presidents, seventy Rhodes Scholars, eighteen astronauts, and seventy-four Medal of Honor recipients, as well as generals such as Robert E. Lee, Ulysses S. Grant, Douglas MacArthur, Dwight Eisenhower, George Patton, and Omar Bradley. In addition, basketball coach Mike Krzyzewski, actress Janine Turner, three Heisman Trophy winners, actors, and Fortune 500 company CEOs are all members of the "Long Gray Line."[95]

Having served as a member of the staff and faculty at West Point for five years, I experienced the inner workings of this leadership development model firsthand. Graduates of West Point have gone on to successful endeavors and careers in every imaginable organizational structure. As noted above, the foundation of the WPLDS is the ideal goal of character development.

The intent of this session is to review and adapt several components of the WPLDS and to apply these principles with the

---

[93] Ibid., 7.

[94] Ibid., 9.

[95] Wikipedia, accessed December 7, 2014, www.wikipedia.org/wiki/United_States_Military_Academy_alumni.

goal of producing leaders of character within any organization. Upon graduation, West Point fully expects graduates to function with efficiency and integrity in each respective assignment, as either officers or members of the army team.

The organizational structure of the US Army is similar to any other organization, with senior, midlevel, and junior or new leaders. Senior-level leaders at Walmart are not asked to lead their employees into battle in Afghanistan, and midlevel leaders at Home Depot are not required to prepare an operations order for deployment to Iraq. The same principles of character development taught at West Point, however, are applicable in business and in life in general. Concentration on and application of the principles in this session will help produce the same results that West Point experiences with each graduating class—producing leaders of character for America and organizations around the globe.

PART I

DEVELOPMENT OF INTELLECT

The person of intellect is lost unless they unite with
energy of character.
                    —Sébastien-Roch Nicolas Chamfort

Intellectual development is simply about learning. Intellectual
development in the West Point model is designed as well to impart
knowledge about how individuals, organizations, cultures, and
societies behave and meet challenges. Further, the model helps leaders
understand the complexity and ambiguity of change over time. The
insights gained from the process of intellectual development are
then applied to the decision-making process, in which leaders must
become proficient. The keyword in this portion of the session is
learning. The idea is that leaders must acquire the ability to master
change by gaining and retaining new knowledge.

For example, Henry Ford's Model T made its debut in 1908 with
a purchase price of $825.[96] The average price of a 2020 Ford Fiesta
today is between $14,260.00 and $21,340.[97] The automobile industry
changed over the years by introducing newer, better-equipped cars
because of public demand. Change is inevitable, and it is important

---

[96] "Henry Ford Changes the World, 1908," EyeWitness to History.com, accessed
December 27, 2014, http://www.eyewitnesstohistory.com/ford.htm.
[97] https://www.zigwheels.us/new-cars/ford/fiesta#:~:text=Ford%20Fiesta%20
2020%20is%20a,%2421%2C340%20in%20the%20United%20States, accessed
September 30, 2022.

to note that change occurs with or without our permission. If the necessity to change is not understood, it is possible that, like Henry Ford's Model T in 1908, we will be left behind, with little awareness of how to lead in a pluralistic society because we rely on outdated knowledge.

The dictionary provides a very interesting definition for the word *change*. One definition is "to make the form, or nature of something different from what it is or from what it would be if left alone."[98] As human beings, we were created to be social beings; we need each other. If, in fact, we need each other, we must also learn from one another. Intellectual development informs the leader of the necessity of this social interaction because there is no organization that will succeed in anything without an understanding of its team members or employees. No one possesses all knowledge. To be a leader of character, the acquisition and retention of new knowledge requires active engagement with a purposeful process of learning.

Leaders learn many lessons from the past—some painful and disappointing, others encouraging and triumphant. What one learns and gains from the pursuit of developing intellectually will write the future of his or her life, beginning with the *writing* of a personal manuscript.

According to the WPLDS, intellectual development is the process of gaining and retaining new knowledge. Developing intellectually asks the question, "What have I learned today that will make me a better leader tomorrow?" The lessons learned about others today have the potential to create an uncommon loyalty among those people a leader leads and will make a difference in someone's future, beginning with the leader's own.

---

[98] "Change," The Free Dictionary, accessed July 17, 2015, http://www.thefreedictionary.com/change.

PART II

DEVELOPMENT OF DISCIPLINE

Success in life comes when you simply refuse to give
up, with goals so strong that obstacles, failure, and loss
only act as motivation.

—Jacqueline Gomez

This phase in the WPLDS focuses on the doctrinal or military
foundation for commissioned service as an officer, or officership.
Officership consists of four facets: warrior, leader of character,
servant of the nation, and member of the profession of arms.
Cadets' perspectives are broadened by participation in experiences
that challenge their current views and expose them to different
worldviews.[99]

An officer is also one appointed or elected to a position that
includes the responsibility or authority to command or direct.
Although this developmental phase at West Point focuses primarily
on the emphasis of military battle doctrine for officers, the perspective
in this session is to take the military battle doctrine focus and capture
it in the principle of discipline—possessing a *military mindset*. In this
sense, the emphasis of a military mindset or discipline is to focus
on the "fight" involved in daily tasks and assignments within any
organization, with the drive to win every day.

---

[99] *Building Capacity to Lead* (New York: United States Military Academy, West
Point, 2009), 3.

The key to winning the daily fight is *discipline*. In business, undisciplined conduct and behavior lead to bad decisions that may cause others to lose money or their jobs. In the military, undisciplined conduct and behavior may lead to bad decisions that may cause others to die.

The dictionary defines discipline as "training to act in accordance with prescribed rules." It further defines discipline as "the rigor or training effect of experience through adversity." Discipline is also described as "behavior in accord with rules of conduct maintained by training and control."[100]

In the foreword of *Leadership Lessons from West Point*, Jim Collins said, in essence, that to be disciplined entails beginning with a framework of core values (*be*), amalgamating those with knowledge and insight (*know*), and finally, making situation-specific decisions to act (*do*). Thus, leadership begins not with what you do, but with who you are (character).[101]

The concepts of "be, know, do," which were first introduced to soldiers in 1983, remain the cornerstone of the core leader competencies (attributes and values that soldiers must *be* and *know*, along with competencies every leader must *do*). "Be, Know, Do" was published first in Field Manual 22-100, which evolved to Field Manual 6-22, published in October 2006, which has continued its evolution into the current Army Doctrine Publication 6-22, published in August 2012, which is not so much a departure from earlier versions of army leadership doctrine as an expansion of them.[102]

With today's all-volunteer force, at the core of being military-minded or developing discipline is an oath of enlistment that assists in establishing the fidelity and integrity of what it means to be an army leader. The oath of enlistment for a new army leader is as follows:

---

[100] Accessed September 30, 2022. https://www.dictionary.com/browse/discipline

[101] Doug Crandall, ed., *Leadership Lessons from West Point* (San Francisco: Jossey-Bass Publishers, 2007), xiv.

[102] Cynthia Patton and Dave Black. "Define the Core Concepts of Army Leadership Doctrine," Army Leadership FM 6-22, Lesson Plan for (ELO) Lesson 6-22-1, 5.

I_____, having been appointed a (rank) in the United States Army, do solemnly swear or affirm that I will support and defend the Constitution of the United States against all enemies, foreign and domestic; that I will bear true faith and allegiance to the same; that I take this obligation freely, without any mental reservation or purpose of evasion, and that I will well and faithfully discharge the duties of the office upon which I am about to enter. So help me God.[103]

September 11, the wars in Iraq and Afghanistan, the ongoing threats from al-Qaeda and ISIS (Islamic State in Iraq and Syria), and terrorist threats around the world have catalyzed the continued evolution of Army Leadership Doctrine. The oath of office is declared by commissioned officers and Department of the Army civilians upon accepting their respective responsibilities to the United States Army and being accountable to our nation in doing their duty. To "do" (conduct) one's duty against all enemies, both foreign and domestic, it is imperative that the first two aspects of what we are to "be" (character) and what we are to "know" (competencies) are established clearly and are practiced in our philosophy of leadership.

General George Washington, commander in chief of the Continental Army during the American Revolution and the first president of the United States, said,

Nothing is more harmful to the service, than the neglect of discipline; for that discipline, more than numbers, gives one army superiority over another.[104]

---

[103] Center for Army Leadership, *The United States Army Leadership Field Manual: Battle Tested Wisdom for Leaders in Any Organization* (San Francisco: McGraw-Hill, 2004), 21.

[104] https://www.afspc.af.mil/News/Commentaries/Display/Article/252573/lessons-on-discipline-from-military-forefathers/, accessed September 30, 2022.

Four-time Olympic gold medalist Jesse Owens once stated, "We all have dreams. But in order to make dreams come into reality, it takes an awful lot of determination, dedication, self-discipline, and effort."[105] Each day brings a set of unique and different challenges to be accomplished. Yet it is a military mindset of discipline or response to act in accordance with the rules prescribed for personal progression that overcomes any and all challenges presented. For Jesse Owens, it was overcoming the challenges of segregation and racism to earn his place in the history books at the 1936 Berlin Olympics. Had it not been for discipline and the actions and rules that Owens had prescribed for himself, he would have been unable to overcome the obstacles and challenges of his day.

In honor of his discipline, forty years later, in 1976, President Gerald R. Ford bestowed upon Owens the Medal of Freedom, the highest civilian honor awarded by the United States, signaling to the world that the man, Jesse Owens, had transcended the invisible obstacles of all things racial to become a galvanizing, ethnic role model for an entire nation.[106]

Further, discipline or a military mindset may be described as "behavior in accordance with rules of conduct maintained by training and control." Training and control have the potential to build confidence for staying the course that discipline has charted.

As George Washington stated, "The neglect of discipline, more than numbers, gives one army superiority over another." A military mindset of discipline does not mean that one has to be in the military to operate by this principle. It means rising to a level of superiority in the pursuit of extraordinary discipline. To be superior is "to be above the average in excellence, a higher place, or position, greater in quality."[107] The pursuit of superiority in discipline suggests surviving the battlefield of everyday organizational challenges where others

[105] "Jessie Owens quotes," Thinkexist.com, accessed December 17, 2014, http://thinkexist.com/quotes/jesse_owens.

[106] https://www.u-s-history.com/pages/h3746.html, accessed September 30, 2022.

[107] https://www.dictionary.com/browse/superior, accessed September 30, 2022.

may not have the drive to do so. A superior, disciplined mindset overcomes any and all obstacles to the organization's mission.

Every company is in business to achieve financial success; if not, it will not be in business long. In an article written for *Forbes*, "Five Reasons 8 out of 10 Businesses Fail," Eric Wagner stated that many fall short of truly remarkable success because of self-sabotage, which results from extremely poor decision-making and weak leadership skills.[108]

Discipline is behavior in accordance with rules of conduct, maintained by training and control. Despite numerous defeats on the battlefield, questionable political allies in Congress, unforgiving weather, and crucial supply demands, the behavior and conduct by the inculcation of discipline (training and control) of Washington's Continental Army was the stimulus for transformation. It was the pursuit and application of discipline in his army that ultimately enabled Washington to defeat the British and win independence for the American colonies.

It is an uncompromising application of discipline to the task or assignment that ensures that any organization wins, despite obstacles, past or present. Coach Vince Lombardi of the Green Bay Packers called discipline "character in action."[109] George Washington and Jesse Owens were two leaders who mastered this principle of discipline in their respective occupations and professions and demonstrated character in action. When we master the principle of discipline, there is no obstacle or challenge that cannot be overcome. Whether we choose to be an author, soldier, athlete, songwriter, or stay-at-home mom, when we practice and apply discipline, we win in all of our chosen endeavors.

---

[108] Eric Wagner, "Five Reasons 8 Out of 10 Businesses Fail," *Forbes*, accessed December 21, 2014, http://www.forbes.com/sites/ericwagner/2013/09/12/five-reasons-8-out-of-10-businesses-fail.

[109] https://www.mentaltoughness.partners/mental-toughness-character-action/, accessed September 30, 2022.

PART III

SOCIAL DEVELOPMENT

If the internet connects us all, then why are so many
of us becoming increasingly isolated?
—Stephen Richards

For the purposes of this session, *social development* is defined as improving the wellness of every individual in the organization so they can reach their full potential. Further, social development is the purposeful investment in people that requires the removal of barriers so that all citizens have the opportunity to grow, develop their own sets of unique skills, and contribute to their families and communities in meaningful ways.[110] In this portion of the session, the keyword or element is *value*. In the WPLDS, the goal of social development is the expansion of one's perspective, both socially and culturally.

As individuals, cadets come to West Point rooted in their own social and cultural perspectives. Some may come from a very small-town environment, where life was calm and quiet, while other cadets may come from the bright lights of a major metropolitan city. As future leaders, their abilities to relate to soldiers from every walk of life are critical to the influence they will have as leaders.

---

[110] https://www.westpoint.edu/sites/default/files/pdfs/ABOUT/
Superintendent/Developing%20Leaders%20of%20Character%202018.pdf,
accessed September 30, 2022, pg. 23.

Social development provides cadets with the ability to form positive, cooperative relationships with others. The WPLDS model uses several methods for this development, including community events, family, philosophical and faith groups, cadet clubs, and teams, all of which shape each cadet's core values and beliefs, identity, and worldview.[111]

It is important to recognize that many social issues still plague our society. Social barriers can take many forms; as stated earlier, social development is an investment in people that removes barriers of any sort. There is no room for discrimination of any kind toward women or people of different races, religions, or ethnic origins. This is why social development is vital in creating a leader of character who values investing in people. This is the process of socialization at its best. Socialization is defined as "a continuing process whereby an individual acquires a personal identity and learns the norms, values, behavior, and social skills appropriate to his or her social position."[112]

The socialization process of these future army leaders in the WPLDS is critical to understanding the importance of building relationships of trust and respect for others cross-culturally, as the United States clearly is a multiracial society.[113] Michel Crevecoeur's often-quoted and adopted metaphor of America as a melting pot simply does not work because it never considered minorities.[114] According to US Census figures, by 2042, minorities will become the majority and will make up more than half of the US population. By 2050, 54 percent of the population will be minorities.[115]

---

[111] *Building Capacity to Lead* (New York: United States Military Academy, West Point, 2009), 5.

[112] "Socialization," Dictionary.com, accessed January 16, 2015, http://dictionary. reference.com/browse/socialization.

[113] Juanita Tamayo Lott, "Do US Racial/Ethnic Categories Still Fit?" *Population Today* (January 1993): 6–7.

[114] https://www.pbs.org/race/005_MeMyRaceAndI/005_01-transcripts-04. htm#:~:text=The%20idea%20of%20the%20melting,not%20melt%20into%20 the%20pot, accessed September 30, 2022.

[115] https://www.cnn.com/2008/US/08/13/census.minorities/#:~:text=But%20 by%202042%2C%20they%20are,all%20children%20will%20be%20minorities,

Having served over twenty-seven years in the army, I recall many leaders, both enlisted and officer, who never understood that it is cultural diversity that strengthens the unity of the organization.

The current recruiting motto for the US Army is "What's Your Warrior?" The army's intent is to reach potential future soldiers and their influencers with relevant, inspiring, and highly engaging content.

The nature of this initiative is designed to address the misperceptions of "military service and a growing disconnect between the army and American youth."[116] A warrior suggests a fight for the standard of right or wrong in life. A person's culture represents, to a large extent, the journey from social norms to societal acceptance. A mutual respect for a person's cultural identity provides a solid platform for the relationship between the leader and the team member as warriors, fighting for right. Each branch of America's armed forces stands upon core values that are vital to morale, good discipline, and the socialization process among its constituents.

The US Navy Core Values:

- **Honor:** Standing tall; caring about your impression on others; doing what is hard because you know it is right.
- **Courage:** Not just courage when the battle is in front of you but courage to do the right thing when no one is watching.
- **Commitment:** To your shipmates, your family, your responsibilities, and to yourself.[117]

---

accessed September 30, 2022.

[116] Army Enterprise Marketing Office, "What's Your Warrior?" Stand-To, https://www.army.mil/standto/archive/2021/01/12.

[117] "Navy Core Values: Born over 200 years ago … The Navy Endures," BootCamp4Me, accessed January 16, 2015, bootcamp4me.com/navy-core-values.

The US Marine Corps Values:

- **Honor:** This is the bedrock of our character. It is the quality that empowers Marines to exemplify the ultimate in ethical and moral behavior: never to lie, cheat, or steal; to abide by an uncompromising code of integrity; to respect human dignity; and to have respect and concern for each other.
- **Courage:** The heart of our Core Values, courage, is the mental, moral, and physical strength ingrained in Marines that sees them through the challenges of combat and the mastery of fear, and to do what is right, to adhere to a higher standard of personal conduct, to lead by example, and to make difficult decisions under stress and pressure. It is the inner strength that enables a Marine to take that extra step.
- **Commitment:** Commitment is the spirit of determination and dedication found in Marines. It leads to the highest order of discipline for individuals and units. It is the ingredient that enables constant dedication to Corps and country. It inspires the unrelenting determination to achieve victory in every endeavor..[118]

The United States Air Force Core Values:

- Integrity First
- Service Before Self
- Excellence In All We Do [119]

Airforce.com provides the following information: The US Air Force core values are much more than minimum standards. They remind us what it takes to accomplish a mission. They inspire us to do our

---

[118] United States Marine Corp Homepage. https://www.marines.com/life-as-a-marine/standards/values.html#:~:text=OUR%20VALUES,and%20fight%20with%20as%20well. Accessed October 25, 2022

[119] United States Airforce Homepage. https://www.airforce.com/mission/vision. Accessed October 25, 2022.

very best at all times. They are common bonds among all comrades in arms and the glue that unifies the Force and ties the great warriors and public servants to the past.

The core values of the armed forces embody the idea of dedication and commitment to the mission. Further embedded in the spirit of these values is the necessity to be able to depend upon one another. The values of an organization are an integral component in developing cohesion and oneness through respect for those values and for each person as a valued member of the team. Social development in the West Point model is designed to enhance the "expansion of one's perspective, both socially and culturally." Social development is a value that cannot be underestimated.

Applying the principle of social development contained in this portion entails the recognition that it is people, not technology, who make companies and businesses go and grow. All people have *value*, and when they are confident that they are *valuable* to the organization and those they follow, you can be assured of their best efforts on a daily basis.

PART IV

MORAL AND ETHICAL DEVELOPMENT

Your actions define your character, your words define your wisdom, but your treatment of others defines the *real* you.

—Mayur Ramgir

"A cadet will not lie, cheat, steal, nor tolerate those who do." The preceding is the Cadet Honor Code, which forms a basis for identifying and examining moral issues at West Point and beyond.[120] The Cadet Honor Code proclaims the standards of integrity expected of all West Point cadets and graduates. The ideals affirmed in the Honor Code attract to West Point young men and women who aspire "to live above the common level of life." The requirements of the Code instruct, motivate, and ultimately shape Cadets during their years at the Academy. Most importantly, effects of the Code continue to guide and inspire graduates during their years of military service and beyond. More than any other aspect of West Point, the Honor Code unites the "Long Gray Line" of Cadets and graduates by expressing their shared commitments to personal integrity and professional responsibility." .[121]

---

[120] "Educating Future Army Officers for a Changing World," Office of the Dean (New York: United States Military Academy, West Point, 2007), 59.
[121] United States Military Academy, West Point. West Point Cadet Honor Code and Honor System.https://www.westpoint.edu/military/simon–center–fo

The Cadet Honor Code is designed to be easy to understand and meet; it is the expected baseline behavior of cadets. The ideal is the daily application of the spirit of the Code, an affirmation of the way of life that marks true leaders of character. In adopting the spirit of the Honor Code, one accepts and applies the principles of truthfulness, fairness, respectability, accountability, and responsibility. This extends beyond external adherence to rules; it is an expression of integrity and virtue manifested in the actions of the honorable man or woman. Those who accept the spirit of the Code think of the Honor Code as a set of principles by which to live, not as a list of prohibitions by which they are hindered.

From this perspective, the keyword is *commitment* to moral and ethical living. Without commitment, society cannot function as it should. In fact, no relationship or organization can function without commitment. Jobs and tasks within businesses can be accomplished efficiently only if workers are committed. Businesses can retain good employees and leaders only when management (leadership) is committed to the welfare of each team employee.

No organization—no matter how large, wealthy, or important— can exist permanently if people within that organization do not make the commitment to operate within a moral, ethical framework.

The professional military ethic is another component of the moral and ethical development of cadets (emerging leaders) at West Point. General Raymond T. Odierno, Chief of Staff, US Army, is quoted in *The Army Ethic White Paper*:

> The foundation of our profession is centered on trust … it will take every measure of competence and commitment to forge ahead and above all, it will take character.[122]

---

r-the-professional-military ethic/honor#:~:text=The%20Cadet%20Honor%20Code%20reads,code%20will%20be%20held%2

[122] Center for the Army Profession and Ethic, *The Army Ethic White Paper,* July 11, 2014.

Raymond F. Chandler III, Sergeant Major of the US Army, is quoted in the same report:

> Being an Army Professional means a total embodiment of the Warrior Ethos and the Army Ethic. Our Soldiers need uncompromising and unwavering leaders. We cannot expect our Soldiers to live by an ethic when their leaders and mentors are not upholding the standard. These values form the framework of our profession and are nonnegotiable.[123]

The army ethic emanates from its foundational heritage, beliefs, traditions, and culture. General Odierno wrote the foreword for *The Army Ethic White Paper*, in which he said:

> Professionals are guided ... This is their identity. Likewise, as Army professionals, [leaders] perform [their *Duties*] according to [their] Ethic. Doing so reinforces *Trust* within the profession and [among those we serve.] [124]

Leadership has and always will be about service to others.

In most professions, people are promoted based on their perceived potential for greater responsibilities within the organization. As senior-level leaders, General Odierno and Sergeant Major Chandler spoke of standards, duty, and trust, none of which can be compromised when living by and maintaining the professional army ethic.

For the purposes of this chapter, the dictionary definition of *standards* is "the morals, ethics, and habits established by customs, traditions, and authority." Standards are defined further as the

---

123 Ibid.
124 Ibid.

"authoritative or recognized exemplar of quality or correctness."[125] If no standards exist, there will be no success.

The Cadet Honor Code, the professional military ethic, and duty, honor, and country are all standards for success in leadership that may be applied in any organizational setting. General of the Army Douglas MacArthur, who spoke to cadets at the US Military Academy when he accepted the Sylvanus Thayer Award on May 12, 1962, likened his award to a "symbol of a great moral code."

In his speech to the corps of cadets that day, MacArthur stated, "Duty, honor, country: those three hallowed words reverently dictate what you ought to be, what you can be, what you will be."[126] In essence, General MacArthur was saying that duty, honor, and country are the foundations upon which your character will be developed for the rest of your life and in service to our nation. A lifelong commitment to moral and ethical development positions the leader to be credible and trusted by those they serve who have made a decision to follow. These same codes of conduct also provide a foundation for service to one's customers, employees, or constituents.

As a former ethics instructor at the United States Army and Armor Center and School in Fort Knox, Kentucky, I will never forget a ten-minute graduation speech by a retired major general from the Vietnam era. One look at his uniform as he walked into the auditorium made it clear that he was a war hero.

In his speech to the graduating class of army second lieutenants, he said, "If your soldiers trust you, they will charge hell with an empty water pistol for you." A leader committed to moral and ethical development inspires this kind of trust—trust that will ensure the standards of the organization are upheld and respected.

---

[125] "Standards," Online Etymology Dictionary. https://www.etymonline.com./search?q=standard&ref=searchbar_searchhint. Accessed October 25, 2022.

[126] The Leadership Forge. It's About "Duty, Honor, Country": Lead with Power of Your Values. http://theleadershipforge.com/2016/06/duty-honor-country-lead-power-values/. Accessed October 25, 2022.

PART V

DEVELOPMENT OF THE HUMAN SPIRIT

We are not human beings having a spiritual experience.
We are spiritual beings having a human experience.
— Pierre Teilhard de Chardin

The goal of this element of the model is to expand cadets' and leaders' perspectives on the imperative of developing the human spirit. Perhaps another way to express the same idea is the development of "one's humanity towards humanity."[127] The key word here is *understanding*. The West Point model holds that the human spirit is developed and sustained by the following five attributes or character strengths:

- **Self-awareness**: reflection and introspection
- **Sense of agency**: ownership, commitment, and engagement
- **Self-regulation**: control of emotions, thoughts, and behavior
- **Self-motivation**: expectancy, hope, optimism
- **Social awareness**: respect, empathy, compassion, transcendence, and communication skills[128]

---

[127] *Building Capacity to Lead* (New York: United States Military Academy, West Point, 2009), 24.
[128] Ibid., 4.

Self-awareness offers the way to discover core values, shape identity, strengthen character, and create perspectives that allow a person to understand his or her experiences and the world. Through reflection and introspection, developing leaders gain insights into some of life's most profound questions, such as, who am I? What is my purpose in life? What is a life worth living? Who do I want to become? What can I believe in? How do I live a life that will make a difference? How can I be happy and content?[129]

The answers to questions of this nature cannot be assumed or presumed if one is to be a leader of authentic character. Answering these introspective and reflective questions helps form and shape one's identity and perspective of the world.

In addition, self-awareness involves having a clear perception of your personality, including your strengths, weaknesses, thoughts, beliefs, motivation, and emotions. Self-awareness allows you to understand other people—how they perceive you—as well as your attitudes toward and responses to them in the moment. Thus, leaders learn who they *really* are as they interact with and receive feedback from their social environment and human interactions.

Second, a *sense of agency* involves assuming ownership or responsibility for one's own spiritual development and a sense of confidence that one has the ability to undertake this developmental quest successfully. Individuals who assume responsibility for such development and engage purposefully in activities that foster their spiritual growth tend to live satisfying and contented lives. In contrast, leaders who fail to take responsibility for their spiritual development are forced to live with the worldviews that society shapes for them, which can cause distress and self-imposed myopia with respect to the reality of the rest of the world in which they live.[130]

The third attribute of *self-regulation* provides cadets with the

---

[129] Colonel Patrick J. Sweeney, LTC, Sean T. Hannah, and Don M. Snider. *The Domain of the Human Spirit in Cadet Development at West Point* (New York: United States Military Academy, West Point, 2007), 7, accessed January 1, 2015, http://isme.tamu.edu/ISME07/Snider07.html.

[130] Ibid., 8.

ability to understand and control their thoughts, emotions, and behavior, which thereby enhances their sense of responsibility and management.[131] In its original Latin form, *regula*, the word *regulate* means to "govern by restriction or to move in a straight line."[132] Therefore, the idea of self-regulation carries the meaning of integrity engendered by self-imposed restrictions (on thoughts, behaviors, and emotions), which direct conduct in a straight line.

The fourth character strength, *self-motivation*, involves the leaders' expectancy, optimism, and hope. Through practice of this character strength, leaders gain an appreciation of and the satisfaction of knowing that living by their values, seeking developmental opportunities actively, engaging consistently in reflection, and working continuously to manage their emotions, actions, and anxieties will develop them into officers capable of leading soldiers in any circumstance or situation.[133]

The fifth aspect is *social awareness*. Social awareness is important in the development of the human spirit because without respect and empathy, a person will have trouble forming connections with other people, which, in turn, will hinder the ability to form new relationships and gain new knowledge about diverse cultures and ideas. Without such experiences, little expansion or refinement of one's worldview is possible.[134]

Hope and faith also are important to note in the development of the human spirit. A leader who inspires the human spirit by increased levels of hope and faith enables team members to imagine future states of self. This, in turn, produces a stronger motivation toward the actualization of becoming respected leaders of character. Thus,

---

[131] *Building Capacity to Lead* (New York: United States Military Academy, West Point, 2009), 4.

[132] "Regulate," Online Etymology Dictionary, accessed July 18, 2015, http://www.etymonline.com/index.regular.

[133] Ibid., 4.

[134] Colonel Patrick J. Sweeney, LTC, Sean T. Hannah, and Don M. Snider. *The Domain of the Human Spirit in Cadet Development at West Point* (New York: United States Military Academy, West Point, 2007), 9.

hope and faith are primary sources of self-motivation in character development. Hope and faith provide people with the willpower to continue to work toward the goal of bolstering and behaving in accordance with their character, even in the face of social pressures to do otherwise.[135] *Webster's* defines *faith* as follows:

> Something that is believed, especially with strong conviction; allegiance to duty or to a person; a firm belief in something for which there is no proof; complete trust; or fidelity to one's promises

Such faith is critical because it provides the direction and will to persist in the continuous and often arduous journey of life and the trust and hope that the journey will produce a life worth living. This includes accepting the reality of the life-or-death implications of military service. It is inevitable—in combat or even in times of peace—that someone will die.

Personal faith is that aspect of the human spirit that sustains confidence for today and hope for tomorrow, even in times of death and dying. This kind of faith is personal; it is a person's confident belief in and commitment to a lifelong quest to develop and to live in accordance with his or her values and principles and to be true to self and not be swayed by the actions and opinions of others.

At the interpersonal level, this type of faith provides a strong sense of conviction or expectancy for the future. It further undergirds the fact that living by our own values and principles and continuously refining knowledge of the inner self through reflection and introspection will make us better leaders. This kind of faith helps us strive to develop our full potential by seeking out new knowledge and experiences and by working for noble pursuits that have a positive influence on others in the organizations we serve. It develops positive relationships with family, friends, and associates, as

---

[135] International Institute for Spiritual Leadership, accessed April 27, 2015, http://iispiritualleadership.com/wp content/uploads/2012/10/CharacterDevelThruSL.pdf.

well as giving us an appreciation and respect for others that will result in enjoying the experiences of truth, happiness, fulfillment, and—if one so believes—the rewards of eternal life. This is the kind of faith that transforms the human spirit.

The world in which we live is more multicultural and multiethnic than it has ever been. The ability to lead in a diverse world is absolutely essential for the accomplishment of today's assignments and tasks, both in the military and civilian sectors. We must expand or develop our perspectives concerning the essence of this domain, at the center of which are our identities, core values and beliefs, and perspectives on how we view the world. The intent is to influence how we act, as well as influencing how we, as leaders, think and feel about any given assignment or responsibility.

It may seem elementary, but the question that must be asked and answered sometimes is this: what does it mean to be human? The word *human* originates from its Latin root *humanus*, which connotes "of man, also humane, philanthropic, kind, gentle, polite; learned, refined, civilized." The word human is also related to *homo*, which means the same: from its modern Latin root, it technically means a "man, or male human."

In logical and scholastic writing, however, it has taken on the meaning of "human being."[136] Therefore, we can rightly say that a human being is a humane being, one who is refined and civilized.

The word *spirit* has several meanings that are important to this session. In its Latin origin, spirit (*spiritus*) means "a breathing, respiration; breath of God." Spirit is defined further as "inspiration; breath of life; disposition, character; vigor, courage; or pride." Another definition of the word is "the soul or heart as the seat of feelings or sentiments," or "the vital animating force within living beings; the part of a human being associated with mind, will, and feelings; and the essential nature of a person."[137] According to this

---

[136] "Human." Online Etymology Dictionary. https://www.etymonline.com./search?q=human, Accessed October 25, 2022.
[137] Colonel Patrick J. Sweeney, *The Domain of the Human Spirit in Cadet Development at West Point*, accessed December 23, 2014, http://isme.tamu.edu/ISME07/

definition, the human spirit influences how we think, act, and feel about life. Thus, the development of the human spirit should form the cornerstone of every leader's development program, including early childhood development. The development of the human spirit at an early age plants seeds of self-worth and self-value that enable a person to view himself or herself as valuable and to view others as valuable as well.

The key word in the human spirit domain is *understand*, a compound word constructed from the words *under* and *stand*. To understand simply means to "stand under." When you stand under a structure, that structure covers or shelters you. The structure in developing the human spirit—encapsulated in self-awareness (reflection and introspection), a sense of agency (ownership and commitment), self-regulation (emotions, thoughts, and behavior control), self-motivation (hope and optimism), and social awareness (respect, empathy, compassion, transcendence, and communication skills)—assists and covers the process of creating leaders of character. Only if these character traits are cultivated within the human spirit will justice and right conduct prevail. It is character strength, such as the preceding, that becomes timeless truth, which will help change people's lives perpetually.

Part of the West Point model's success in developing leaders is that throughout the years, decision-makers at the academy have recognized that change is constant and continual. Therefore, a strategy for character development must also be constant and continual.

The final portion of this session is a brief adaptation of the expansion of the West Point model of character development, published in December 2014.

Snider07.html.

PART VI

FIVE FACETS OF THE
WEST POINT CHARACTER
DEVELOPMENT STRATEGY

The foundation of the five facets of the character development strategy is to establish honorable living within the emerging leader's life. As described earlier, developing the intellect and discipline; developing socially, morally, and ethically; and developing the human spirit are all connected to this latest strategy at West Point. As it has been for over 213 years, the intent remains the same. The strategy is designed to influence and create a mindset of honorable living in graduates that guides conduct and behavior or the establishment of authentic character.

The five facets of the strategy are as follows:

- Moral
- Performance
- Civic
- Leadership
- Social [138]

---

[138] The William E. Simon Center for the Professional Military Ethic, *Character Development Strategy* (New York: United States Military Academy, West Point, December 2014), 9.

Facet 1—Moral

It is important to note that although they are often used interchangeably, there is a difference between ethics and morals. *Ethics* refer to rules provided by an external source (e.g., codes of conduct in workplaces or principles in religions). *Morals* refer to an individual's *own* principles regarding right and wrong. It is possible to adhere to a code of ethics and be immoral or amoral. When leaders are *immoral*, they are prone to making decisions that violate societal standards or those of the organization to which they belong. When someone is *amoral*, he or she has no morals and either does not know what right or wrong means or does not care about moral behavior.

A review of West Point's moral facet illustrates the development and responsibility for both moral and ethical behavior for the emerging leader. The army values of loyalty, duty, respect, selfless service, honor, integrity, and personal courage merge with the professional army ethic of how a soldier and leader behaves twenty-four hours a day, seven days a week. The practical expression of this first principle comes to life in the performance aspect of the strategy.

Facet 2—Performance

The second facet within the strategy, *performance*, indicates urgency or simply getting the job done. It is an understanding of the fact that the organization depends on a leader of a certain caliber to accomplish the task, despite obstacles or difficulties. It is a partnership in which everyone contributes to accomplishing the mission assigned. It is a mindset that it must be done.

Facet 3—Civic

The *civic* facet addresses the idea of responsibility to one's workplace or community. This facet includes leader attributes such as dignity, respect, empathy, and loyalty to others or the ideal of a genuine display of caring for people. Another way to think about this facet is to genuinely *care* for people, as seen in the following acronym:

- **C**onsiderate
- **A**ltruistic
- **R**efreshed
- **E**ncouraging

Considerate: To be considerate in communication, I must consider the effect or influence upon others in what I am about to do or say. Considerate communication shows an uncommon level of respect that is unsurpassed by outward circumstances or situations. This is the place of acquired *maturity*. Maturity does not refer to rank or age; it is wisdom in judgment, the quality of being able to make the right call or decision (effect or influence).

Altruistic: An altruistic leader carries consideration to a higher degree. Altruism is the opposite of selfishness. Contrary to popular belief, the most dangerous fish in existence is not the Amazonian piranha or the great white shark. The most dangerous "fish" in existence is "selfish." The altruistic leader not only does for others without any expectation of reward but also may sacrifice to do so. The altruistic leader's focus is to benefit others.

Refreshed: No matter how practiced and efficient an organization or company may be, throughout the course of its existence there always is a need to be refreshed and promoted at every level of leadership. Days off, vacations, or a change of pace are ways to become refreshed. To be refreshed simply means to give new strength and energy, to stimulate and revive. We live in a society where we change the motor oil in our automobiles every three thousand miles and rotate our tires between three thousand and six thousand miles. Caring leaders are those who recognize when and how to give the people they lead some time for self-maintenance, lest they break down. The leader also is not exempt from the need to be refreshed.

Encouraging: The prefix *en* means "to add." The civic-minded leader, therefore, purposefully plans to enhance others' courage.

Courage involves overcoming fear, which includes the fear of failure. This is achieved by support, confidence, hope, and assurance, all of which the leader employs to encourage those he or she leads. In this light, to encourage is to lift up another by believing in that person, even through setbacks or failures. Every person who has succeeded in a chosen profession also has experienced setbacks and failure. To fail does not make a person a failure. The lessons that we learn from setbacks or failures have the potential to shape our professionalism. These leaders learn and grow because tomorrow is on the horizon, and the organization depends upon them to do their parts. An encouraging leader helps everyone do his or her part, even in setbacks and failures that make them all better leaders.

Facet 4—Leadership

Leadership is the glue that holds everything together. The ability to inspire and achieve results while protecting the welfare of those they lead is the essence of leadership in this facet. To inspire is to "put spirit in." To do so, the leader must *be* inspired—and influential as well. To be inspirational also is to be motivational. Through consistent modeling, we show others why we are in our chosen profession. This type of leader does not settle for the status quo but instead challenges people never to settle for good when better or best still may be achieved.

Authentic leadership is established in purposeful relationships. This includes the ability to create environments of value, trust and respect. These purposeful actions provide synergy, confidence, and a mindset that creates greater productivity among those who follow. In this facet, being in a position of leadership does not always equate with being a leader. Those who follow will always know a leader whose behavior is consistent with the substance of this facet. It is incumbent upon emerging and senior leaders to maintain their focus on this facet and never lose sight of the importance of growing better and stronger in leadership every day. In so doing, the desired results will always be accomplished.

Facet 5—Social

This facet relates to the representation or mindset of professionalism in any social environment or interaction with people. As described in the preceding facets, a person of character is always the standard-bearer of the organization in all interactions with people because it is true that we have only one opportunity to make a first impression. Yet when we belong to a particular organization, the impression that people will receive from that interaction is not only personal but potentially can be organizational. Some will wonder, "What kind of company or organization condones bad manners or a lack of social etiquette?"

Bad manners or conduct and inappropriate speech destroy the image of the values of an organization; therefore, it is the goal of this facet to instill social competence. Cadets (emerging leaders) are trusted to be professional and representatives of the US Army as leaders of character, whether they are in uniform or on leave on a beach in the Caribbean. Character is inseparable from leadership in any social environment or interaction with people. From this perspective, the impression that a leader of character makes will leave an indelible imprint in society that is distinct and commendable and that others will want to emulate.

In any organizational setting, application of the WPLDS principles, combined with the five facets of character development, will assist leaders at every level to achieve and maintain excellence in productivity, product, and service to the people of their company and community by operating in the spirit of *duty, honor, country.*

Summation: Proven Principles of Character Development

For over two hundred years, West Point has produced leaders of character. This is not to say that this model is the only one that will produce such leaders, but throughout the history of the institution, lessons have been learned that have helped to continue to create the types of leaders for our armed forces and society that will continue to make a difference in leader development. In other words, the principles have been proven.

The West Point experience of leader development is a proven four-year developmental process with the overarching goal of graduating commissioned officers who are warriors, leaders of character, and servants of the nation. The entire model focuses on developing in cadets the knowledge, skills, and competencies that are critical in establishing the professional practice of an army officer and fostering continued growth as a strategic thinker and leader. As cadets develop intellectually, militarily, socially, morally/ethically, and spiritually, the intent is to release, to the army and our nation, men and women of unquestionable character. The inculcation of the five facets of the West Point Character Development Strategy (WPCDS) woven into the fabric of the existing Cadet Leadership Development System is the path, or method, by which the mission of the academy is accomplished.

The mission statement of the United States Military Academy (USMA) is:

> To educate, train, and inspire the Corps of Cadets so that each graduate is a commissioned leader of character committed to the values of 'Duty, Honor, Country,' and is one who is prepared for a career of professional excellence and service to the nation as an officer in the U.S. Army.

Adopting or adapting these proven principles of character development has the potential to make and raise the level of character in any organization. It will require commitment and discipline that will challenge every leader and employee to understand that the practice of and investment in character development is worth it.

> Two things define you. Your patience when you have nothing and your character when you have everything.
>
> —George Bernard Shaw

Questions for Reflection

1. Which of the five elements of the adapted WPLDS discussed in this session (intellectual, discipline, social, moral-ethical, and human spirit) would be the most profitable to your organization, and how would you use your selections to develop your employees or team members?

2. What changes would you make in your organization to establish a mindset of discipline to the organization's goals that is beyond the ordinary?

3. In the domain of the human spirit, what practical steps do you take to live a life that will make a difference in the hearts and minds of those who follow you?

4. Using the five key words in each part of this session (learn, discipline, value, commitment, understanding), what approach would you use to create a leadership development process for those you lead?

5. The civic facet of the West Point Character Development Strategy includes dignity, respect, empathy, and loyalty. Considering this facet on a scale of one to ten, with ten as the highest, how would you rate your organization's operational effectiveness, according to this principle? If the score is low, what could you do to raise it?

Quotes of Principled Leaders

"Duty, Honor, Country"—those three hallowed words reverently dictate what you ought to be, what you can be, what you will be. They are your rallying point to build courage when courage seems to fail, to regain faith when there seems to be little cause for faith, to create hope when hope becomes forlorn.

—General Douglas MacArthur

A true leader has the confidence to stand alone, the courage to make tough decisions, and the compassion to listen to the needs of others. He does not set out to be a leader, but becomes one by the equality of his actions and the integrity of his intent.

—General Douglas MacArthur

Make us to choose the harder right instead of the easier wrong, and never to be content with a half-truth when the whole can be won.

—West Point Cadet Prayer

Leadership is a potent combination of strategy and character. But if you must be without one, be without the strategy.

—General Norman Schwarzkopf

Leadership is the art of getting someone else to do something you want done because he wants to do it.

—Dwight D. Eisenhower

Moral courage is the most valuable and usually the most absent characteristic in men.

—General George S. Patton Jr.

SESSION IV

THE OTHER SIDE OF FAILURE

> It's fine to celebrate success but it is more important
> to heed the lessons of failure.
>
> —Bill Gates

Foundation

After graduating from high school in the Detroit Public School System in 1976 and after obtaining several advanced degrees, I cannot recall taking one class or learning one lesson on the reality of failure. This spans approximately forty years, and I cannot recall one organizational environment (public school system, college, or military) that discussed failure. Perhaps this is because failure is not an easy topic to discuss in our success-oriented society. It may be our own emotional experiences, embarrassment, and/or perceived perceptions from others that make this topic difficult to discuss. Dictionary.com defines failure as "a lack of success; a subnormal quantity or quality; an insufficiency."

People, companies and organizations of all types, athletes and professional sports teams, Hollywood actors, musicians, and recording stars all focus their attention—and rightly so—on success, not failure. Many programs discuss success or how to be successful in a particular vocation or occupation, but there are not many consistent platforms for learning or discussing success through failure. It is inevitable and inescapable that failure will occur, both personally and in every organization.

In 1711, Alexander Pope, in "An Essay on Criticism," stated, "To err is human; to forgive is divine."[139] Herbert V. Prochnow paraphrased Pope slightly by saying, "To err may be human, but to admit it isn't."[140] Error is defined as "a deviation from accuracy or correctness." It is also defined as "a mistake in action." Pope helps us understand that we *all* make mistakes, and those mistakes have the potential to lead to failure in some task or assignment.

Prochnow provides us with the mindset that many have, regardless of successes and failures. To admit personal or organizational failure is, in some instances, counterproductive to one's future. Most of us have heard the saying, "Failure is not an option." What lies beneath this lofty ideal is the motivation to succeed.

For Winston Churchill and the people of Great Britain, failure was not an option! The survival of their nation and their way of life was dependent upon overcoming the attacks of Hitler and Nazi Germany. In many instances, however, failure must and *needs to be* an option to discover the truest way to success. No one wants to fail or to be labeled a failure.

Success is the goal of every responsible leader, team member, and reputable organization. For those who have experienced any level of success, there also has been significant failure that taught them valuable lessons of endurance and perseverance.

Winston Churchill. As a two-time Nobel Prize-winning, twice-elected prime minster of the United Kingdom, Churchill was not always as well regarded as he is today. He struggled in school and failed the sixth grade. After school, he faced many years of political

[139] Grammatist. "To Error is Human To Forgive Is Divine." https://grammarist.com/proverb/to-err-is-human-to-forgive-divine/. Accessed October 25, 2022.
[140] Natalie D. Breacher. Gale Academic Onefile. "Latin Lessons: Admitting Fault Can Save The Day." https://go.gale.com/ps/i.do?p=AONE&u=googlescholar&id=GALE|A303474455&v=2.1&it=r&sid=googleScholar&asid=07d88254

failure, as he was defeated in every election for public office before, he finally became the prime minister at the age of sixty-two.[141]

Vincent Van Gogh. During his lifetime, Van Gogh sold only one painting—to a friend and for only a very small amount of money. While Van Gogh was never a success during his life, he continued to paint, sometimes starving to complete his over eight hundred known works. Today, Van Gogh's paintings are worth hundreds of millions of dollars.[142]

Stephen Spielberg. While Spielberg's name today is synonymous with highly successful, big-budget films, he was rejected from the University of Southern California's School of Theater, Film, and Television three times. Eventually, he attended school elsewhere, only to drop out to become a director. Spielberg directed such movies as *E.T.*, *Jurassic Park*, *Jaws*, *Schindler's List*, *Raiders of the Lost Ark*, and *The Color Purple*, to name just a few. Spielberg's net worth today is approximately $3.6 billion. Thirty-five years after starting his degree, Spielberg returned to school in 2002 and finally earned his BA.[143]

Soichiro Honda. Honda said,

> When I started making motorcycles, the prophets of doom, some of them my friends, came to discourage me. "You'd be better off opening another garage, in the country, or in Tokyo. You'll make a lot of money. There are a lot of cars that need to be repaired in this country." I didn't listen to them, and despite their pessimistic advice, I created, on the 24th of September, 1948, next door to my research laboratory, the Honda

[141] Wikipedia. Winston Churchill. https://en.wikipedia.org/wiki/Winston_Churchill. Accessed October 25, 2022.
[142] Britannica. Vincent Van Gogh. https://www.britannica.com/biography/Vincent-van-Gogh. Accessed October 25, 2022.
[143] Britannica. Stephen Spielberg. Stephen Spielberg. https://www.britannica.com/biography/Steven-Spielberg. Accessed October 25, 2022.

Motor Company, which today is a billion dollar business.

Honda also stated that his biggest thrill "is when I plan something and it fails. My mind is then filled with ideas on how I can improve it. When you fail, you also learn how not to fail."[144]

Walt Disney. In 1922, Disney and a partner started their first film company in Kansas City, Kansas. The two men bought a used camera and made short advertising films and cartoons under the studio name Laugh-O-Gram. Disney even signed a deal with a New York company to distribute the films he was producing. That arrangement didn't work out, though, as the distributor cheated the studio. Without the distributor's cash, Disney couldn't cover his overhead, and the studio went bankrupt in 1923.

Disney was once fired by a newspaper editor because he "lacked imagination and had no good ideas." Disney left Kansas City for Hollywood, and it was there, in 1928, that a new character named Mickey Mouse made his debut.[145] Today, the Walt Disney Company and its subsidiaries and affiliates are worth approximately $143 billion. This includes consolidated subsidiaries, such as ESPN, Disney Channels Worldwide, ABC Family, and the SOAPnet networks. In addition, it operates ABC, ESPN, ABC Family, and SOAPnet-branded internet businesses, as well as the ABC Television Network and television stations and the ESPN Radio Network and Radio Disney Network, and it owns and operates radio stations. The Parks and Resorts segment owns and operates Walt Disney World Resort in Florida and the Disneyland Resort in California. In addition to the theme parks in America, there are Tokyo Disney, Disneyland

---

[144] "Soichiro Honda Quotes," Quoteswise.com, accessed April 26, 2015, http://www.quoteswise.com/soichiro-honda-quotes.html.

[145] Way4vision. "The Man Who Love To Do The Impossible-Walt Disney." https://way4vision.wordpress.com/2016/07/04/the-man-who-love-to-do-the-impossible-walt-disney/. Accessed October 25, 2022.

Paris, and Disneyland Hong Kong.[146] All of this was created by a man who had failed initially because he "lacked imagination and had no good ideas."

Elvis Presley. Even decades after his death, Elvis is a household name as one of the best-selling artists of all time. Back in 1954, however, Elvis was still a nobody. Jimmy Denny, manager of the Grand Ole Opry, in Nashville, Tennessee, fired Elvis Presley after just one performance, telling him, "You ain't goin' nowhere, son. You ought to go back to driving a truck."

Michael Jordan. Most people wouldn't believe that a man often lauded as the best basketball player of all time was actually cut from his high school basketball team. Jordan didn't let this setback stop him from playing basketball. He stated,

> I have missed more than 9,000 shots in my career. I have lost almost 300 games. On 26 occasions, I have been entrusted to take the game-winning shot, and I missed. I have failed over and over and over again in my life. And that is why I succeed.[147]

Vera Wang. In 1968, Wang tried out but failed to make the cut for the US Olympic figure-skating team. She later became an editor for *Vogue* magazine, only to be passed over for the editor in chief position. Wang later began to design wedding dresses and now has a billion-dollar industry![148]

[146] Forbes, Accessed December 2, 2014, http://www.forbes.com/companies/walt-disney.

[147] Advantage. Talent Development Tuesday. https://www.advantageperformance.com/talent_development/the-power-of-failure/. Accessed October 25, 2022.

[148] "WSJ. Magazine April 2015: The Columnists," WSJ Magazine, accessed April 26, 2015, http://www.wsj.com/articles/vera-wang-brian-grazer-and-more-on-failure-1427468012.

The preceding examples of the road from failure to success suggest that in order to move forward, you have to decide to *keep moving*. Understand that this is often easier said than done. As leaders, we must face the facts of our failures and keep moving forward. Considering that some type of failure has occurred, assess *what* happened and *how* it happened and *take* corrective measures to see that it does not happen again (even though it may); just keep moving forward. *Failing does not make you a failure.*

PART I

FAILING DOES NOT MAKE YOU A FAILURE

Only by knowing yourself can you become an effective leader.

—Vince Lombardi

For the legendary coach Vince Lombardi, one of the most important aspects of his players' performance was the value of knowing themselves. When considering players to add to the team roster, a football or basketball coach will send scouts to view a perspective player to determine the strengths and weaknesses of that particular player. The scouts analyze the potential player further to see if he or she would fit well into their team's system or style of play. The scout's perspective is based on observation, while the players' perspectives of playing at the college or professional level concerns what they *believe* about themselves.

Whether on the football field or in the corporate boardroom, knowing oneself is essential to success. Believing in oneself and knowing one's capabilities and potential are the foundations of personal and organizational success. It is a leader's internal awareness, drive, and motivation that help him or her realize that when a failure occurs, it must be separated from self. Coach Lombardi's point is that by knowing yourself when the failure occurs, you know internally that you are not a failure, and this is what makes you an effective leader.

J. K. Rowling. J. K. Rowling, the author of the *Harry Potter* series, was invited to be the graduation speaker at Harvard in 2008. Rowling didn't talk about success. She talked about failures—her own, in particular. Rowling told her audience, "It is impossible to live without failing at something, unless you live so cautiously that you might as well not have lived at all—in which case, you fail by default."

Initially, twelve publishers rejected the first *Harry Potter* manuscript before the first book was published in June 1997. Today, over 400 million copies of the books have been sold worldwide, and they have been translated into sixty-seven languages. The Harry Potter brand is valued at over $15 billion, making Rowling the first billionaire author[149]

Colonel Harland Sanders. According to his 1974 autobiography, before Harland Sanders became a world-famous Colonel, he was a sixth-grade dropout, a farmhand, an army mule-tender, a locomotive fireman, a railroad worker, an aspiring lawyer, an insurance salesman, a ferryboat entrepreneur, a tire salesman, an unsuccessful political candidate, a gas station operator (where he also served food to travelers), a motel operator, and, finally, a restaurateur.

When he was sixty-five, a new interstate highway snatched the traffic away from his Corbin, Kentucky, restaurant, and Sanders was left with nothing but a Social Security check and a secret recipe for fried chicken. After over one thousand rejections of his secret recipe for chicken, he finally persuaded Pete Harman in South Salt Lake, Utah, to be his partner. They launched the first Kentucky Fried Chicken site in 1952. In 1955, confident of the quality of his fried chicken, the Colonel devoted himself to developing his chicken

---

[149] Insider, Judith Aquino. "The Brilliant Methods That Made Harry Potter A $15 Billion Dollar Brand." https://www.businessinsider.com/jk-rowling-business-methods-2011-7#:~:text=Fourteen%20years%2C%20seven%20books%20and,Rowling%20the%20first%20billionaire%20author.Accessed. October 25, 2022.

franchising business. Less than ten years later, Sanders had more than six hundred KFC franchises in the US and Canada.

Until he was stricken with fatal leukemia in 1980 at the age of ninety, the Colonel traveled 250,000 miles a year, visiting KFC restaurants around the world.[150] As of December 2020, there are twenty-five thousand KFC outlets in 145 countries and territories around the world. Kentucky Fried Chicken is currently worth over $23 billion.[151]

Larry Page, Sergey Brin, and **Google**. In 1995, Larry Page and Sergey Brin met at Stanford University when they were graduate students in computer science. By January 1996, the pair had begun to collaborate in writing a program for a search engine dubbed BackRub, named after its ability to do back-link analysis. Next, fueled by BackRub's rave reviews, Page and Brin began working on Google. Operating out of their dorm rooms, the pair built a server network using cheap, used, and borrowed PCs. The partners reached their credit card limits in buying terabytes of discs at discount prices. Page and Brin then tried to license their search engine technology but to no avail. After failing to find anyone who wanted their product in its early stages of development, the two decided to keep Google, seek more financing, improve the product, and take it to the public themselves. As of May 2022, Google is worth almost $1420 billion.[152]

Mario Andretti. From the time that he was a young boy, four-time Indy Car National Champion Mario Andretti always lived life in the fast lane. After stepping away from his racing career in the mid-1990s, at age fifty-four, he translated his philosophy for winning races to business:

---

[150] Kentucky Fried Chicken, accessed November 26, 2014, http://www.kfc.com/about.

[151] *Iconic Global Brand* (Louisville: Yum Brands, 2014), 98.

[152] Caknowledge.com. https://caknowledge.com/google-net-worth/. Accessed October 25, 2022.

Surround yourself with the top people in the field, make sure they have the necessary tools to do their jobs, go out there to win each time, and don't fear failure.[153]

Andretti stated further:

Desire is the key to motivation, but it is determination and commitment to an unrelenting pursuit of your goal—a commitment to excellence—that will enable you to attain the success you seek.[154]

Each of the preceding examples provides an illustration of believing in yourself and that the pursuit of what you believe is valuable. How you see yourself will determine what you believe about yourself. The glass is never half empty, even in times of failure; it is always half full, and a leader who understands this is determined to keep moving forward. What you think of yourself is more important than what others may think of you. Although some of the men and women in our preceding examples experienced significant rejection and failure, they were all determined to persevere. An unrelenting pursuit of their goals and passions, their belief in themselves, and their true commitment formed the bridge that led these men and women to become history-making leaders when they reached the other side of failure—success.

---

[153] Success, accessed April 26, 2015, http://www.success.com/article/mario-andretti-a-glass-half full-for-the-indy-500-and-formula-one-champion.
[154] "Career Highlights," Mario Andretti, accessed November 28, 2014, http://www.marioandretti.com/career-highlights.

PART II

PURSUE EXCELLENCE, NOT PERFECTION

Perfection is not attainable, but if we chase perfection, we can catch excellence.

—Vince Lombardi

Vince Lombardi was born in Brooklyn, New York, in 1913. As head coach and general manager of the Green Bay Packers, Lombardi led the team to three NFL championships and to victories in Super Bowls I and II in 1967 and 1968.

Because of his success, he became a national symbol of single-minded determination to win. Under Coach Lombardi's no-nonsense leadership, the struggling Packers were transformed into hard-nosed winners. Over the course of his career with the team, he led the club to a 105-35-6 record and five championships, including three straight titles from 1965 to 1967. The team never suffered a losing season under the Hall of Fame coach.[155] Lombardi believed that leaders are made, not born: "They're made by hard effort, which is the price all of us must pay to achieve any goal that is worthwhile."[156]

---

[155] "Vince Lombardi," Biography, accessed November 23, 2014, http://www.biography.com/people/vince-lombardi.

[156] Famous Quotes By Vince Lombardi. http://www.vincelombardi.com/quotes.html. Accessed October 25, 2022.

In an article titled "Pitfalls of Perfection," Hara Marano stated, "Concern with mistakes and doubts about actions are absolute prerequisites for perfectionism." Perfectionists fear that a mistake will lead others to think badly of them; the performance aspect is intrinsic to their view of themselves. Concern with mistakes is a reflection of what one professor calls the core issue in perfectionism: the unspoken belief or doubt that arises and says, "I'm incompetent or unworthy."[157] Marano said in her article that experts now know that perfectionists are *made*, not born, commonly at an early age. They also know that perfectionism is increasing. One reason is that many parents base much of their status on the performance of their children.[158]

In the article, Marano shared the thoughts of one Northeast College student who said, "My parents were perfectly happy to get Bs and Cs when they were in college. But they expect me to get As." Many of today's parents are not only overly involved in their children's lives, but they demand perfection from them in school.

Parents who demand perfection, as well as employers who demand perfection from their employees, create a recipe for unnecessary stress and distress. Perfectionism creates a pervasive personality style that becomes a way of life for those who have been shaped and molded by its pattern.[159] Being raised in such an environment leaves no room, psychologically or socially, for a child to know that it is all right to make mistakes. Consequently, perfectionist behaviors and attitudes follow the individual into adulthood, a cycle that often continues in the workplace and creates an unrealistic approach to tasks or assignments.

In learning from our mistakes, we learn what does and does not work to produce the desired results. Perfectionism produces a steady source of negative emotions. Rather than reaching toward something positive, those in its grip are focused on the very thing they most want to avoid—a negative evaluation of self. A mistake is sometimes

---

[157] Hara Estroff Marano, "Pitfalls of Perfection," *Psychology Today* (March 1, 2008), http://www.psychologytoday.com/articles/200802/pitfalls-perfectionism.
[158] Ibid.
[159] Ibid.

simply a misunderstanding or an error in action. As stated in the foundation of this session, an error is defined as "a deviation from accuracy or correctness," and as "a mistake in action." Perfectionism allows only for perfection. If perfection is the standard, then anything less than perfection equates to the possibility of failure, rather than a lesson in learning. The pursuit of excellence, however, carries an entirely different meaning from that of the pursuit of perfection.

Although Lombardi was a disciplined leader, his perspective in all of his championship years with the Green Bay Packers was not the perfection of his team but the pursuit of excellence. Lombardi's Jesuit training in spiritual disciplines at Fordham University, as well as the five years he spent at West Point, is what helped forge his leadership philosophy.[160]

In addition to this foundation, the Jesuits taught Lombardi that character and will are linked forever in a virtuous cycle so that character superimposed upon the will produces character in action.[161] By example and deed, Coach Lombardi worked to make winners on the football field and in life through character in action. By the team's learning the plays and their repeated execution of what they had learned, Coach Lombardi's pursuit of excellence is what made his a winning team. Although mistakes were made in practice and in the games, it was not perfection for which Coach Lombardi asked but excellence—he knew that it is impossible to attain perfection in an imperfect world. Human beings make mistakes and errors in judgment.

Computers are susceptible to viruses and hackers, which contradicts the idea that technology is perfect. The dictionary defines *perfection* as the "state or quality of being or becoming perfect. To be perfect is to be complete beyond practical or theoretical improvement. Accurate, exact, or correct in every detail."

In contrast, *excellence* is defined as "a state of excelling, or

---

[160] David Maraniss, *When Pride Still Mattered: A Life of Vince Lombardi* (New York, New York: Simon & Schuster Publishers, 1999), 101.

[161] Westside Toastmasters, accessed November 22, 2014, http://westside toastmasters.com/resources/communication_secrets.

superiority." To be excellent is "to possess outstanding quality or superior merit, or to be remarkably good." By its very definition, perfection or perfectionism disregards the fact that we are human. No one is capable of perfection, but everyone is capable of excellence. As stated before, the largest room in the world is the room for improvement.

Every year, Ford, Honda, Mercedes-Benz, and the automobile industry in general provide us with the latest models of their cars. They tell us of the improvements they have made in each vehicle that comes from their factories and why it is the best car on the market.

The computer and cell phone industries advertise their newest personal computers, tablets, and cell phones and tell us why we need them. We're grateful for those who understand and recognize the need for constant evaluation and improvement of those things that make life and work more convenient for us. Every few months, there are new models of washing machines, appliances, and gadgets to purchase. It is a constant cycle of new and improved innovations.

In this cycle, we invest ultimately in what we choose to believe. Our automobiles, homes, and the technology that we choose are all indicators of what we believe in. Businesses or hotels that have existed for many years sometimes pause to consider the value of renovations in their existing buildings, the infrastructure of their staff, and their philosophy of operation. To renovate is simply to "improve upon what you have or to make new." While some would say that there's nothing wrong with being old school, change takes place whether we agree with it or not. Change is inevitable, just as is failure.

If one is a perfectionist, it is possible to begin the process of changing one's perspective from perfectionism to quality performance or excellence. T. Alan Armstrong once said,

> If there is no passion in your life, then have you really
> lived? Find your passion, whatever it may be. Become

it, and let it become you and you will find great things happen for you, to you, and because of you.[162]

To be passionate about success provides the motivation for excellence, even in the face of failure. Passion for excellence is both admirable and inspirational. When this passion is practiced personally, others in the organization are affected positively. This type of attitude spreads quickly and produces a drive and desire for additional and multiplied success among team members.

Success is also the goal of perfectionism, but it has the potential to isolate and contaminate other team members, which is unhealthy for both the individual and the organization. When we invest in improving ourselves (pursuing excellence, not perfection), it is an indicator that we acknowledge that room for improvement remains.

Coach Lombardi's approach to instilling in his team a championship mindset is embodied in his philosophy: "Perfection is not attainable, but if we chase perfection we can catch excellence." It is the pursuit of excellence and not the pursuit of perfection that carries us to the other side of failure, which is success. When we fail, as is inevitable, how we approach the situation either impedes or expedites the learning process. One means of doing so is by operating with the principle of "stepping back to step forward."

---

[162] Think Exist.com, accessed November 30, 2014, http://thinkexist.com/quotation/if-there-is-no-passion-in-your-life.

PART III

STEP BACK TO STEP FORWARD

> Once you agree upon the price you and your family must pay for success, it enables you to ignore the minor hurts, the opponent's pressure, and the temporary failures.
>
> —Vince Lombardi

Most of us remember learning how to ride a bicycle and every aspect of the experience. You may even recall the number of times you fell off your bicycle before you learned how to balance yourself. Although you may have fallen several times, the pleasure of riding your bicycle outweighed the pain that you experienced in falling off. With our parents' help or your own single-mindedness, you were trained—or you trained yourself—how to ride a bike. Similarly, in every vocation, a certain amount of training is required. This training can last anywhere from one week to many years, depending upon the expertise necessary.

Training is necessary to acquire the basic knowledge needed to perform the job for which a person has been hired. In any given situation, when people are trained well, they develop the ability to respond, not react. A basic definition of *respond* is to "act favorably." For the purposes of this section, to *react* means to "act in a reverse direction or manner."[163]

When confronted with the inevitability of failure, a leader who is

---

[163] "React." https://www.dictionary.com/browse/react. Accessed October 25, 2022.

trained to respond rather than react will take a step back in order to step forward. As defined in the foundation of this session, failure is "a lack of success, a subnormal quantity or quality; an insufficiency."[164] A leader who has been trained to step back has developed the ability to separate the moment from the momentum. A leader who has been trained to step back in order to step forward has developed the ability to separate himself or herself from the circumstances by accepting reality, acknowledging responsibility, and acting resolutely. The *moment* is the time frame and the way in which the lack of success or insufficiency (failure) occurred. For our purposes, *momentum* is defined as the power to move.

Accepting reality, acknowledging responsibility, and acting with resolve is a part of the training that keeps us from being moved by the momentum or power of our emotions and other people's perspectives or opinions of us in the moment. The investment we make in developing the ability to respond or to act favorably is of incalculable value when failure occurs. To *react* is to act in a reverse manner or direction, while our training to *respond* favorably to failure begins by acknowledging reality.

Acknowledge Reality

In the moment that failure occurs, take a step back to step forward by acknowledging reality. Remember that because you have failed at a particular assignment or task does not make you a failure. To step back means to respond *favorably*, rather than *emotionally*, to the failure in a given assignment. Understandably, responding favorably in the moment may be quite challenging, but this is the reason why soldiers train for war in peacetime. It will certainly be a battle in itself to control negative emotions, such as disbelief, detachment, or self-condemnation. To respond favorably to the moment is to know for oneself that the glass is half full and not half empty.

Although someone may say that you have failed at a particular

---

[164] Ibid.

task or assignment, the key is to know for yourself that you are not a failure. Responding favorably means that you don't deny that it has happened or ask how it could happen to you. It has *happened* and may happen again if you do not learn from the moment. In the school of hard knocks, a lesson learned is knowledge earned. Deal with the reality of the moment and the reality of the momentum or the power to be moved by your emotions. Do not personalize or internalize the matter. Embrace the fact that there is no success without failure—and you are not a failure.

Accept Responsibility

One way to define responsibility is *having the ability to respond*. For the leader of character, the goal is always to respond positively, not negatively, to the moment. The ability to respond is the capacity and competency to act favorably to correct an insufficiency or lack of success. When failure occurs in the workplace, and the boss looks for answers, many quickly adopt a defensive posture to deflect blame.

A leader of character, however, never plays the blame game. Accepting responsibility also suggests that the leader has a choice, and it addresses the maturity of the leader or particular team member. The choice that you have as a mature member of the team is not to blame anyone else. Defensiveness and blame destroy cohesion and lead to separation and alienation. A mature member of the team is committed to the success of the organization and its future. The success of the organization is also the success of the team. Theodore Roosevelt once said, "If you could kick the person in the pants responsible for most of your trouble, you wouldn't sit for a month."[165] If you are given the responsibility, then you also must walk in accountability.

To be accountable means to be *answerable*. As leaders of character, we are accountable to the team to which we belong and to the larger

---

[165] "Personal Responsibility Quotes," Good Reads, accessed December 5, 2014, http://www.goodreads.com/quotes/tag/personal-responsibility.

organization of which we are members. Accepting responsibility means that we must discover the root of the failure, look failure in the face, and respond favorably to what we have done or not done.

It was said of Thomas Edison that he, like other inventors, possessed faith, courage, persistence, and responsibility for his acts. "I've tried everything. I have not failed. I have just found 10,000 ways that won't work!"[166] Edison went on to hold more than one thousand patents and invented world-changing devices, such as the phonograph, the electric lamp, and the movie camera. Acknowledging reality and accepting responsibility for failure are the cornerstones of success. It is just the starting point, however, not the finish line. The lessons of the journey are not yet complete, as we must act with resolve.

Act Resolutely

After acknowledging reality and accepting responsibility for failure, the key to success is to act with resolve, which requires us to move forward patiently and persistently. The nature or essence of acting with resolve is in getting over the failure and in growing (maturing) as a result of it. What this means further is that we maintain our focus on our purpose. As a young boy, Thomas Edison's teachers told him he was "too stupid to learn anything." He did not have much more success in the workplace, as he was fired from his first two jobs for not being productive. For Edison, this turned a perceived negative into a positive. "If I find 10,000 ways something won't work, I haven't failed. I am not discouraged, because every wrong attempt discarded is another step forward."[167] Despite harsh criticism, at some point in his youth, Edison discovered and made the decision to maintain his focus on his purpose.

A person who acts with resolve dispels any doubts or fears of

---

[166] Ibid.

[167] Amethyst Tate, "Celebs Who Went from Failures to Success Stories," CBS News (July 19, 2012), http://www.cbsnews.com/pictures/celebs-who-went-from-failures-to-success-stories.

moving forward. Resolve is to "settle, or determine, by deliberate action, will power, and intention, regardless of failures to move forward." Resolve is a leadership attribute that undergirds maintaining the focus of one's purpose.

Whether with Vince Lombardi's Green Bay Packer championship teams or any other such team, the principle remains the same. Every player on a championship team is charged to maintain his or her focus on the purpose—and the purpose is to win. This is the mindset of the successful. For Coach Lombardi's teams, whether an offensive or defensive player, whether a quarterback or a safety, each had a specific role that every other member of the team counted on to fulfill *individually* to benefit the team *collectively*. The quarterback is not asked to perform the role of the safety. The safety is not asked to function as a wide receiver.

A resolute leader decides what is important and determines to fulfill his or her role, even when things go wrong or meet with little success. Success simply doesn't happen without failure. The question that we must ask is, how bad do we want to achieve our purpose? For the resolute leader, the motivation must be sufficient to prevent failure or rejection from derailing his or her resolve. A Japanese proverb says that if you fall down seven times, get up eight. It becomes a personal matter of how much we believe in what we are doing. It is my choice to believe.

Steve Jobs, the founder of Apple, dropped out of college after one semester. He also quit one of his first jobs to backpack around India and, according to CNN, admitted using psychedelic drugs. Jobs later said that these experiences helped him create the largest technology company in the world. At the time of his death in 2011, Jobs's net worth was $8.3 billion.[168]

Nelson Mandela spent twenty-seven years in prison before becoming the first president of South Africa in a fully representative democratic election. During his time in jail, he kept a scrap of paper

---

[168] "Steve Jobs Fast Facts," CNN, accessed April 26, 2015, http://www.cnn.com/2013/08/23/us/steve-jobs-fast-facts.

in his cell that contained the words of a poem by William Ernest Henley, titled "Invictus," which ends with the famous lines: "I am the master of my fate: I am the captain of my soul."[169] A prudent leader learns to embody those two famous lines from "Invictus."

"I am the master of my fate" means choosing to believe in your character, refusing to be dominated by adversity or failure, and knowing that you have the ability to overcome—that is to be "the captain of one's soul."[170]

According to CNN, *The Oprah Winfrey Show* was one of the highest-ranking shows in American history, although Oprah's first employer told her she was too emotional and not right for television. According to *Forbes* magazine, in 2011, Oprah was the highest-paid female in the entertainment industry, and she remains the richest self-made woman and the only African American female billionaire.[171]

Both failure and success are honest and impartial and do not discriminate. Developing the capacity to step back in order to step forward is the ability to move away from the circumstances in which the failure occurred and take positive steps to correct what went wrong. It means to allow neither the moment nor the momentum of our emotions to cloud our ability to remain focused on our purpose. It is by acknowledging reality, accepting responsibility, and acting with resolve, consistently and persistently, that leaders at every level are prepared to handle failure.

The examples of the men and women cited in this session are those of ordinary people who achieved the extraordinary. Through hardship and adversity, each of these people made a decision to maintain their focus on their goal to succeed. These extraordinary

---

[169] Keld Jensen, "Rock Bottom: How Great Leaders Triumph Over Failure," Forbes, accessed April 27, 2015, http://www.forbes.com/sites/keldjensen/2012/08/08/rock-bottom-how-great-leaders-triumph-over-failure.

[170] William Ernest Henley, "Invictus," Poetry Foundation, https://www.poetryfoundation.org/poems/51642/invictus. Accessed April 26, 2015

[171] Amethyst Tate, "Celebs Who Went from Failures to Success Stories," CBS News (July 19, 2012), http://www.cbsnews.com/pictures/celebs-who-went-from-failures-to-success-stories.

achievements were all accomplished despite people's perspectives or perceptions. Our emotions about our mistakes and failures can sometimes be overwhelming.

To build a bridge to the other side of failure, we need the components of the lessons that we have learned. It does not mean that we will not make mistakes; the greatest challenge is not to make *the same mistake* again (although it is possible for it to happen again) or to experience the same failure again.

If we do not learn the lessons in the moment, the momentum of our emotions (power to move) will keep us from growing and progressing toward success. When we develop the right perspective, failure is simply an opportunity to begin again on the other side, which is success.

> You don't learn from successes; you don't learn from awards; you don't learn from being a celebrity; you only learn from wounds and scars, mistakes and failures.
>
> —Jane Fonda

Summation: The Other Side of Failure

No one wants to fail or to be labeled a failure. Success is the goal of every responsible leader, team member, and business. Believing in oneself and knowing one's capabilities and potential are the foundation to personal and organizational success. Internal awareness and motivation allow a leader to separate failure from himself or herself. Leadership is not the pursuit of perfection; rather, it is the pursuit of excellence, which all can attain. Perfectionism, according to Hara Marano, is an endless report card; it keeps people completely self-absorbed and engaged in perpetual self-evaluation, which leads to relentless frustration, anxiety, and depression.

As we have seen in this session, it is impossible to achieve perfection in an imperfect world. The goal of perfectionism also is success, but it has the potential to isolate and contaminate other team members, which is unhealthy for both the individual and organization.

When we invest in improving ourselves (pursuing excellence, not perfection), it is an indicator that we acknowledge that there remains room for improvement. It is possible for a perfectionist to begin the process of changing his or her perspective from perfectionism to quality performance or excellence.

T. Alan Armstrong once said,

> If there is no passion in your life, then have you really lived? Find your passion, whatever it may be. Become it, and let it become you and you will find great things happen for you, to you and because of you.[172]

When confronted with the inevitability of failure, a leader who is trained to respond, not react, will take a step back in order to step forward.

As defined in the foundation, failure is "a lack of success, a subnormal quantity or quality; an insufficiency." A leader who has

---

[172] Think Exist.com, accessed November 30, 2014, http://thinkexist.com/quotation/if-there-is-no-passion-in-your-life.

been trained to step back has developed the capacity to separate the moment from the momentum. A leader who has been trained to step back in order to step forward has developed the ability to step back from the circumstances by accepting reality, acknowledging responsibility, and acting with resolve.

It is important to keep in mind that failure is honest and impartial and does not discriminate. Developing the capacity to step back in order to step forward requires moving away from the circumstances or situations where the failure has been identified and taking positive steps forward to correct what went wrong. It means further to allow neither the moment nor the momentum of our emotions to cloud our ability to maintain focus on our purpose. Being passionate about success provides the motivation for excellence, even when failure has occurred. When confronted with the inevitability of failure, a leader who is trained to respond rather than react will take a step back in order to step forward.

Excellence is defined as "a state of excelling, or superiority. To be excellent is to possess outstanding quality or superior merit, or remarkably good."

By definition, perfectionism denies the reality of being human. No one is capable of perfection; everyone is capable of excellence. The point of this session is that when we allow failure to teach us, and we apply the lessons learned, the other side of failure will always be success.

Questions for Reflection

1. If failure is a reality in life and leadership, how do you prevent members of your team from being emotionally traumatized by the experience, rather than learning lessons from it?

2. What principles from this session can be implemented to safeguard you and your team from the pitfalls of perfection and, instead, have a positive, collaborative mindset to pursue excellence?

3. How would you improve or modify the principle of "Step back to step forward" for your organization?

4. How would you help a team member you are mentoring to overcome mistakes and the criticism of peers so he or she can maintain focus on his or her purpose in the organization?

5. There are members of your organization who have proven that they do not operate by the truths of acknowledging reality, accepting responsibility, and acting with resolve. What course of action could you take to help others (including yourself) discover the need for change?

Quotes of Principled Leaders

The brightest future will always be based on a forgotten past; you can't go forward in life until you let go of your past failures and heartaches.

—Iliketoquote.com

If winning isn't everything, then why do we keep score?

—Vince Lombardi

Mistakes are always forgivable, if one has the courage to admit them.

—Bruce Lee

By seeing the seed of failure in every success, we remain humble. By seeing the seed of success in every failure we remain hopeful.

—Paul J. Meyer

It's never too late to be what you might have been.

—George Eliot

AFTERWORD

THE LEADER'S RESPONSIBILITY
OF ACCOUNTABILITY

At the beginning of the year 2020, I had the opportunity to conduct a leadership conference for a very successful friend and organization with approximately three hundred leaders as a part of his staff. We had lost contact but had served together in leadership development circles over twenty years ago. Within approximately thirty seconds of our conversation after twenty years, he began talking about how frustrated he was with his leadership staff.

There was very little catching up from the past. There was no conversation about how the children were doing or how he was doing, but within the first few seconds of our conversation, this very successful leader went immediately to talking about how frustrated he was with his staff of leaders. Some may think that this is uncommon, but I would submit that it's more common than we are aware or choose to acknowledge.

The challenge for many may be in the question, "With whom can I be open and honest enough as a leader to share my frustrations?" In session one, "Character and Virtue: The Foundations of Authentic Leadership," we discussed that the answer to any leadership crisis, including our own personal and organizational frustrations, is the consistent and persistent development of character and virtue.

Virtues are qualities of moral goodness or excellence. When we speak of individual virtues, we are talking about qualities to which we aspire. Virtues are further regarded as qualities of the mind, the will, and the heart that instill strength of character and stability of personality. I submit that responsibility and accountability are included in virtues to be developed and practiced as a part of the leader's character.

Warren Bennis, distinguished professor of business administration and founding chairman of the Leadership Institute at the University of Southern California, says that the ancient Greek translation of character is "to engrave," and its related noun means "mark or a distinctive quality." Character is who we essentially are, and our character continuously evolves.[173] It does not matter what position of leadership we may hold; leadership is our character, and our character becomes our leadership. One cannot exist without the other.

In this afterword, we will focus on three final concepts of the leader's character: a mindset of responsibility, a mindset of accountability, and a mindset of communication. We begin our discussion with several brief definitions that are relevant to the leader's responsibility of accountability—mindset, principle, precept, and leadership.

Defining a Mindset

Psychologist Kendra Cherry describes *mindset* as,

> A learned tendency to evaluate things in a certain way. These can be evaluations of people, problems, objects, situations, or events. Such evaluations are often positive or negative but can also be mixed or uncertain at times.[174]

---

[173] Josephson Institute, accessed April 24, 2015, http://josephsoninstitute.org/business/resources/poc_bennis_character-leadership.html.
[174] "What is Mindset? Simple Definition & Meaning of Mindset," Happy Rubin, https://happyrubin.com/happiness/what-is-mindset. Accessed May 25, 2020.

Mindset.com defines mindset as "a collection of beliefs and thoughts."

Wikipedia describes mindset in a similar way:

> The collection of beliefs and thoughts that form the (mental) attitude, habits or attitude that predetermines one's interpretations and reactions to events, circumstances, and situations.[175]

I personally define mindset as "a mind that is set on what the mind believes."

Defining a Principle

When we think or speak of a principle at Ethnos Leadership, our definition is, "a universal law that is true in any context, situation, environment or organization." It is much like the law of gravity—we don't have to understand or like the law of gravity, but if we step out of a fifth-story window, we will quickly come into agreement that the law of gravity is true. Therefore, we further think of a principle as truth that transforms a person's or leader's mindset.

Defining a Precept and Leadership

A precept may be defined as "a guiding principle or rule that is used to control, influence, or regulate conduct or behavior."[176] We further define a precept at Ethnos Leadership as "life lessons; words to live and lead by." Ater over forty years of leadership research and development, I have reached the conclusion that if you were to take one thousand people, place them in a room, and ask them to give

---

[175] Ibid.

[176] "Precept," Your Dictionary, https://www.yourdictionary.com/precept. May 25, 2020.

you a one-word definition of leadership, most would choose the word *influence.*

Therefore, we define leadership (influence) as "the capacity to become a compelling, irresistible force, that effects, the actions, behavior, and conduct of others."

A Mindset of Responsibility

The Department of Defense Dictionary of Military and Associated Terms defines responsibility as "the obligation to carry forward an assigned task to a successful conclusion. With responsibility comes authority to direct and take the necessary action to ensure success." [177] Simply put, the practicing and developing leader has the ability to respond. Referencing our definition above, no matter what the organizational setting may be, the leader has been placed in a position of confidence and granted the authority to accomplish a given task successfully.

No organization will place someone in a position of responsibility without trusting or believing that the leader possesses the character and necessary ability for successful accomplishment of a given assignment. What the definition above appears to lack, however, although sound and applicable, is the people element of leadership.

The people element of leadership is referred to in "The What and the Why of Ethnos Leadership" at the beginning of the book. The people element of the leader's responsibility of accountability is noted in the Ethnos Equation of purposeful relationships and authentic accountability, which becomes my professional responsibility. Purposeful relationships are intentional relationships that are valued, trusted, and respected. These types of relationships will not occur unless there is an accompanying mindset concerning the purpose of these relationships. A portion of that purpose is authentic accountability or that which is reliable, dependable, and affirmational.

---

[177] Department of Defense Dictionary of Military and Associated Terms, https://irp.fas.org/doddir/dod/jp1_02-march-2013.pdf. Accessed May 28, 2020

When we speak or talk about being *reliable*, this means the establishment of a reputation for being a leader of consistency, credibility, and believability. In other words, leaders are trusted by those they lead. When we speak of being *dependable*, this means that whoever our leader may be, we are confident that we can come to that leader for continued development, even through our mistakes and failures. This is an incalculable attribute of purposeful relationships. When authentic accountability is established, this removes the roadblock of silence between the leader and the led. Authentic accountability has the potential to create a path of open, honest dialogue and communication that creates a better and more effective work or organizational environment.

The third component of the Ethnos Equation is professional responsibility. The responsible and accountable leader has the assignment to develop those he or she leads, socially, emotionally, spiritually, and physically. These four elements of professional responsibility are intended to continue the cycle of purposeful relationships and authentic accountability.

Socially, we live and lead in a very diverse world. The leader's responsibility of accountability concerning social development includes acquiring certain skills, attitudes, mindset, and behavior that enables the leader to interact with others, respecting the unique strengths that a diverse organization possesses. There once was a time in our society when a person's IQ was the most important aspect of leadership, but since the 1990s, Daniel Goleman's *Emotional Intelligence: Why It Can Matter More than IQ* has proven to be perhaps the greatest ally for creating purposeful relationships, authentic accountability, and professional responsibility, thereby increasing the effectiveness of organizations. Goleman defines emotional intelligence (EQ) as "a person's ability to manage his or her feelings so that those feelings are expressed appropriately and effectively." According to Goleman, EQ is the largest single predictor of success in any organization.[178]

---

[178] Ben Cole, "Emotional Intelligence," TechTarget, https://searchcio.techtarget.com/definition/emotional-intelligence. May 28, 2020.

The leader's responsibility of accountability includes the development of the human spirit as a part of the Ethnos Equation. Development of the human spirit is the place where the ability to overcome hardship, adversity, and the pain that life often brings is practiced and cultivated. The etymology of the word *spirit* suggests origins in the original Latin *spiritus*, which simply means breath.

During a speech at Trinity College, on June 15, 1941, General George C. Marshall declared,

> The soldier's heart, the soldier's spirit, the soldier's soul, are everything. Unless the soldier's soul sustains him, he cannot be relied on and will fail himself, his commander and his country in the end.[179]

As a senior leader, General Marshall addressed the value of a soldier's character, which, for many, includes the faith factor—an unparalleled combat multiplier. The faith factor of a person is to be included and considered as a part of developing the human spirit. A person's religious preference may also be a part of his or her own emotional intelligence.

For some, faith is a great factor; for others, not much at all, but what General Marshall was speaking of, I believe, included the factor of faith and the ability to breathe through the atrocities of war and death.

For some, their hardships, adversities, and the pain that life often brings is included in the same category emotionally. Therefore, the responsible and accountable leader recognizes and understands that by empathizing with whatever hardship and pain a person in their organization is going through, they will get through it together.

The final element of professional responsibility is the physical development of those that we lead. We know that physical activity or exercise can improve our health and thereby improve our quality of life. Yet the aim in the leader's responsibility of accountability is not just physical fitness but also learning how to play hard because

---

[179] The George C. Marshall Foundation, https://www.marshallfoundation.org/library/digital-archive/speech-at-trinity-college. Accessed May 28, 2020.

of how hard we work; it's finding and discovering ways to recharge our batteries. Physical development also includes the development of our family relationships.

Many leaders are gone from home for days, weeks, and sometimes even months at a time. Finding the opportunity to develop their families physically, whether it's going to the swimming pool in the park or playing baseball or softball with their children, is a critical mindset to develop and never forget.

The aim of physical development is certainly physical fitness, but it is also physically developing the strengths and cords of our families because our families are the foundation of who we truly are.

A Mindset of Accountability

"Accountability is a readiness to have one's actions judged by others and to accept responsibility, where appropriate, for errors, misjudgments, and negligence and recognition for competence, conscientiousness, excellence, and wisdom; closely related to the principles of morality, and ethics."[180]

The preceding definition of accountability provides us with insight that is not always easy to discuss. This definition may also suggest that the leader has failed in some respects in completing his or her duties. No leader wants to be in error or to be seen as negligent or incompetent.

The most valuable section of this book—for me, personally, as a leader—is Session IV, "The Other Side of Failure," due to the many times that I have failed. In one of the *Star Wars* movies, Master Yoda hit Luke Skywalker in the head with his cane, saying, "Failure is the best teacher."

---

[180] The Arthur W. Page Center/ Public Relations Ethics. "Ethical Principles of Accountability and Responsibility." https://pagecentertraining.psu.edu/public-relations-ethics-in-crisis-management/lesson-1-prominent-ethical-issues-in-crisis-situations/ethical-principles-of-responsibility-and-accountability/. Accessed May 30, 2020.

"The Other Side of Failure," as you might recall, has three main subheadings that support Master Yoda's viewpoint:

1. Failing Does Not Make You a Failure
2. Pursue Excellence, Not Perfection
3. Step Back to Step Forward

Holding yourself accountable to these principles and precepts will help you to help others who have failed and who don't know how to handle the failure. It is important that anyone who has failed in life and leadership (and that's all of us) learns the lessons of failure that carries them to the "other side," which is success.

In the late 1990s, I served as the ethics instructor at the United States Army and Armor Center, Fort Knox, Kentucky. My responsibility was teaching ethics or moral leadership. While assigned to the United States Military Academy, West Point, as staff and faculty in the early 2000s, I learned that written in the bedrock of a cadet's leadership development is the Cadet Prayer. Both of these seasons of my life and learning provided valuable insight into the leader's character.

The Cadet Prayer, written by Chaplain (Colonel) Clayton Wheat in 1924, helps to communicate West Point's mission:

> To educate, train, and inspire the core of cadets so that each graduate is a Commission leader of character committed to the values of duty, honor, country and prepared for career of professional excellence and service to the nation as an officer in the United States Army.[181]

---

[181] West Point—the US Military Academy, https://www.facebook.com/WestPointUSMA. May 30, 2020.

The Cadet Prayer

O God, our Father, Thou Searcher of Human hearts, help us to draw near to Thee in sincerity and truth. May our religion be filled with gladness and may our worship of Thee be natural. Strengthen and increase our admiration for honest dealing and clean thinking and suffer not our hatred of hypocrisy and pretense ever to diminish. Encourage us in our endeavor to live above the common level of life.

Make us to choose the harder right instead of the easier wrong, and never to be content with a half-truth when the whole can be won. Endow us with courage that is born of loyalty to all that is noble and worthy, that scorns to compromise with vice and injustice and knows no fear when truth and right are in jeopardy.

Guard us against flippancy and irreverence in the sacred things of life. Grant us new ties of friendship and new opportunities of service. Kindle our hearts in fellowship with those of a cheerful countenance and soften our hearts with sympathy for those who sorrow and suffer.

Help us to maintain the honor of the Corps untarnished and unsullied and to show forth in our lives the ideals of West Point in doing our duty to Thee and to our Country. All of which we ask in the name of the Great Friend and Master of all. Amen.[182]

Leaders of character are needed in every office of every organization, no matter the industry or profession to which one belongs. Therefore, the leader's responsibility of accountability

---

[182] "Cadet Prayer," West-Point.org, https://www.west-point.org/academy/malo-wa/inspirations/cadetprayer.html. Accessed May 30, 2020.

includes developing leaders to focus on choosing the *harder right* instead of the *easier wrong.*

It does not matter how small the difference may seem in the eyes of some; know that choosing the harder right instead of the easier wrong, does make a difference because character still matters.

A Mindset of Communication

This final component of the leader's responsibility of accountability, a mindset of communication, is developing the skill set to effectively communicate the principles and precepts of the nature and intent of this book. There is no doubt that we are in the information age. Our cell phones, smartphones, and tablets, with Google's, Alexa's, and Siri's help, make information available to us within a few seconds. To sift through all the information available at a moment's notice and then to communicate it effectively requires a *mindset of communication.*

Merriam-Webster.com defines communication as "the act or process of using words, sounds, signs, or behaviors to express or exchange information or to express your ideas, thoughts, and feelings with others."[183] The word *communication* is derived from the Latin word *communicare*, which means to impart, to participate, to share, or to make common. Communication may be further defined as an interchange of thought or information between two or more persons to bring about mutual understanding and desired action.[184]

Josina Makau, in the book *21ˢᵗ Century Communication: A Reference Handbook*, states,

> Communication is the use of available resources to convey information, to move, to inspire, to persuade,

---

[183] "Communication," Merriam-Webster, https://www.merriam-webster.com/dictionary/communication. Accessed May 30, 2020.
[184] Nadeem Khan, "What Is the Best Definition of Communication?" MBA Notes, https://www.mba-notes.com/2020/06/Definition-of-Communication.html.

to enlighten and to connect which is an inherently ethical undertaking.

Makau's position is that there is a right way and a wrong way to communicate.

Therefore, the ethically effective communicator is a leader who makes his or her exchange of information clear and consistent with the values of the organization's mission. This leaves no room for doubt, cynicism, or distrust because the communication at every level is clear and ethically sound.[185] As we speak, most of us do not think of communication from an ethical perspective; we simply think of what to say in our exchange with others. The chart below provides us with an illustration of some of the dynamics involved in communication.

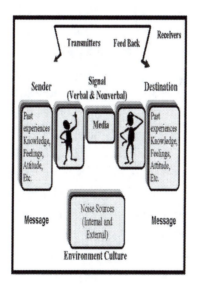

I believe that most of us will agree that all of the above chart is true, even though we do not necessarily think of communication as we're speaking because many times we speak before we think. It is

---

[185] Josina Makau, "Ethical and Unethical Communication," in *21ˢᵗ Century Communication*, ed. William F. Eadie, Accessed May 30, 2020. https://sk.sagepub.com/reference/communication/n48.xml.

important that we remember that the sender, as the initiator of the communication, is always responsible for the accuracy of the message.

Therefore, clear, concise, accurate words and gestures are important to the communication environment. A text message or email is certainly a means of communication, but depending on the message that is sent, sometimes a phone call or person-to-person contact will be more effective. This is all part of the leader's responsibility of accountability.

As the sender of a particular message or effort to communicate, if you have had difficulty communicating with a certain person previously, most likely as you attempt a new communication, the same past experiences, knowledge, feelings, and attitude are not only going to be present with you as the sender but will also be present with the receiver.

Because of the fast-paced and busy lives we live, we seldom think about communication in our exchange of information; we simply speak. Depending upon the organization or culture, some may not ask questions during the staff meeting or exchange of information; therefore, effective communication may be short-circuited. Effective communication is not talking *at* someone but talking *with* someone. If there is no authentic exchange of information, we invite:

- *Mis*interpretation (inaccurate decoding)
- *Mis*communication (no clear exchange of info)
- *Mis*information (inaccuracy of message, missing info)
- *Mis*understanding (no comprehension)
- *Mis*guidance (leads in the wrong direction)
- *Mis*takes (incorrect actions or conduct)

A key to improving our communication skills from this perspective is strengthening our ability to *listen* for comprehension and understanding, not listening by waiting to respond. In the final analysis, the components of clear, effective communication include:

- Time
- Accuracy of message
- Sender
- Medium (method)
- Receiver
- Response
- Feedback (close the loop)

As we practice these attributes as responsible and accountable leaders, our mindsets are focused on being effective communicators, thereby increasing organizational effectiveness and productivity, which subsequently helps to create and concretize satisfied and content people in our organizations.

I will conclude this afterword where it began. I told you the story of a very successful leader who was frustrated with his leadership staff. Leadership is no easy task; it requires a mindset of determination, no matter with what today's leader is confronted. I also suggested at the beginning of this afterword that the answer to any leadership crisis, including our own personal and organizational frustrations, is the consistent and persistent development of character and virtue.

This book is about the leader's character—those who have a virtuous mindset, who are needed today in ways that we could not have imagined. None of us ever could have imagined that American citizens would storm our nation's Capital on January 6, 2021, where a police officer was beaten, a rioter was shot, and three others died during the rampage.[186]

What makes America great are leaders like you—committed to being a leader of character and providing hope for a better tomorrow for our children and our children's children. Your reading this book suggests that you have determined to be a leader of character—always refining your skills on this never-ending journey of leadership

---

[186] Jack Haley. "These Are the People That Died in the Capital Riot." New York Times, January 11, 2021. https://www.nytimes.com/2021/01/11/us/who-died-in-capitol-building-attack.html

development, balancing your position of leadership by investing in people, and making a difference one life at a time.

I am hopeful that we will one day experience what President Dwight D. Eisenhower signed into law on June 14, 1954, concerning our Pledge of Allegiance: "One Nation under God, indivisible, with liberty and justice for all."[187] This is my hope for my children and my children's children and my country.

We are better together, and I'm grateful for the leadership relationship that we now share in the principles and precepts of this book because without a relationship, there is no leadership.

—G. L. Cruell

---

[187] Scott Bomboy, "The History of Legal Challenges to the Pledge of Allegiance, Constitution Daily, https://constitutioncenter.org/blog/the-latest-controversy-about-under-god-in-the-pledge-of-allegiance. Accessed May 31, 2020.

Quotes on Responsibility and Accountability

At the end of the day, we are accountable to ourselves. Our success is a result of what we do.

—Catherine Pulsifer

The day soldiers stop bringing you their problems is the day you have stopped leading them. They have lost their confidence that you can help them or concluded that you do not care. Either case is a failure of leadership.

—Colin Powell

The man who complains about the way the ball bounces is most likely the one who dropped it.

—Lou Holtz

In the long run, we shape our own lives. The process never ends until we die. And the choices we make are ultimately our own responsibility.

—Eleanor Roosevelt

Ninety-nine percent of all failures come from people who have a habit of making excuses.

—George Washington Carver

We are made wise not by the recollection of our past, but by the responsibility for our future.

—George Bernard Shaw

It is wrong and immoral to seek to escape the consequences of one's own actions.

—Mahatma Gandhi

Accountability breeds responsibility.

—Stephen R. Covey

It is not only what we do, but also what we do not do, for which we are accountable.

—Moliere

Responsibility equals accountability which equals ownership. A true sense of ownership is the most powerful weapon a team or organization can have.

—Pat Summit

Wisdom comes from personal accountability. We all make mistakes; own them … learn from them. Don't throw away the lesson by blaming others.

—Steve Maraboli

On good teams a coach holds his or her players accountable. On great team's players hold players accountable.

—Joe Dumars

Anyone that is good for making excuses is seldom good for anything else.

—Benjamin Franklin

The most important thing I learned is that soldiers watch what their leaders do. You can give them classes and lecture them forever, but it is your personal example they will follow.

—Colin Powell

The responsibility is all yours. No one can stop you from being honest and straightforward.

—Marcus Aurelius

For more information about the Ethnos Leadership Process (ELP), please visit us at www.gregorycruell.com, via email at info@ gregorycruell.com, or by phone at (254) 394-3133.

ADDITIONAL BOOKS
BY DR. GREGORY L. CRUELL

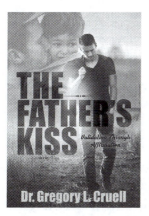

The story of the prodigal son depicts, at one time or another, various phases of life. If you have ever been the victim of bad choices or have been hurt from the past, *The Father's Kiss* is the catalyst for turning personal tragedy into triumph. From *The Father's Kiss*, you will receive grace, reconciliation, restoration, validation, and affirmation. Once you have received *The Father's Kiss*, others will also be "kissed" by the gift and grace of God that your life has become. The impact of the embrace of *The Father's Kiss* will change you and those around you forever.

Many scientists have agreed that the mind is the seat of consciousness and awareness, the essence of our being that further governs our character and behavior. One study reports that the mind thinks between 60,000 and 80,000 thoughts a day. That's an average of 2,500–3,300 thoughts per hour! Other experts estimate 50,000 thoughts per day, which means about 2,100 thoughts per hour. Most agree that over half of our thoughts are

159

negative. Negative thoughts can impact behavior and shape identity. You may be thinking, "I am a positive person. How can I have negative thoughts?" Positive people can have negative thoughts; they just may not express them outwardly. Psychologist William James once stated, "When you alter your thinking, you alter your life." As we alter our thinking, we begin to live brand new lives. Change the way that you think, and you will change your life and the lives of those around you.

From a leadership perspective, character refers to the ethical and moral traits of a person. These traits can be used to assist in giving the leader his or her individuality. The character of a person is evident, no matter what the situation. Behavior can change, but the character or nature of a person does not. This first book of the Ethnos Leadership Process contains the four sessions of the character module that are designed to assist the authentic leader's quest for a lifetime commitment of leadership and mentorship by continuing to discover the limitless dimensions of character development by self-reflection and self-evaluation.

This second book of the Ethnos Leadership Process is designed to pursue and acquire future capabilities that help others to discover that it's never too late to learn what we are capable of. *The Leader's Capabilities* covers "The Art of Communication: Can You Hear Me Now?"; "Conflict: Handle It or It Will Handle You"; "Establishing Values That Unite an Organization"; and "Creating Transformational Leaders That Transform Others." As we focus on the future in the present, we guarantee the solidity of our organizations' heritage and legacy.

The final book of the Ethnos Leadership Process contains the four sessions of the competency's module, or "The Investment Is Worth It." Competence is the capacity to function in one's profession successfully and efficiently. It includes a combination of knowledge, basic requirements (capabilities), skills, abilities, behavior, and attitude. The competent leader also understands the responsibility to pass the baton of leadership by authentic (not casual) mentoring of others. The competent leader is on a never-ending quest of proficiency and mastery of his or her profession for the sake of mentoring others. It is this drive and motivation that has proven to be the key to personal and organizational legacy.

For more information about our books or online courses, visit us at www.gregorycruell.com, via email at info@gregorycruell.com or by telephone at (619) 765-4868.

Printed in the United States
by Baker & Taylor Publisher Services